MEET THE
CANDIDATES
2020

CORY BOOKER

A VOTER'S GUIDE

Series Edited by
SCOTT DWORKIN

Compiled and Written by Grant Stern

Skyhorse Publishing

Introduction copyright © 2019 by Scott Dworkin
Compiled and written by Grant Stern

Skyhorse Publishing books may be purchased in bulk at special discounts for
sales promotion, corporate gifts, fund-raising, or educational purposes. Special
editions can also be created to specifications. For details, contact the Special Sales
Department, Skyhorse Publishing, 307 West 36th Street, 11th Floor, New York,
NY 10018 or info@skyhorsepublishing.com.

Skyhorse® and Skyhorse Publishing® are registered trademarks of Skyhorse
Publishing, Inc.®, a Delaware corporation.

Visit our website at www.skyhorsepublishing.com.

10 9 8 7 6 5 4 3 2 1

Library of Congress Cataloging-in-Publication Data is available on file.

Cover design by Brian Peterson

ISBN: 978-1-5107-5027-2
Ebook ISBN: 978-1-5107-5035-7

Printed in the United States of America

CONTENTS

INTRODUCTION TO CORY BOOKER

BY SERIES EDITOR SCOTT DWORKIN

When Senator Cory Booker decided to run for Democratic nomination for president in 2020, the field wasn't as broad and diverse as it is now. Former vice president Joe Biden, Mayor Pete Buttigieg, Beto O'Rourke, Senator Bernie Sanders, and Senator Elizabeth Warren all had not announced their official candidacies yet. What started as a better playing field for a Booker 2020 campaign has now led to a fight for him to pull up from the bottom. But as you'll learn in this book, out of the candidates running for office, Booker is one of the few I would never count out.

The senator has a mix of grit, determination, and courage combined with positivity, faith, and love. He is selling a bright future, not one that is all doom and gloom. And if he plays his cards right, he might be able to pull off a stunning upset in the primary campaign. Booker is not someone who is just going to roll over and not be competitive. He has always shown that he is willing to go above and beyond what most others would do in whatever role he serves in.

Booker's proven for years that he will do whatever it takes to help his community, even if it causes him bodily harm. In April 2012, "Booker dashed into a burning Newark house next door to his own. When he emerged, Booker had his next-door neighbor in his arms, had second-degree burns, and was suffering from the effects of smoke inhalation," reported the *Washington Post*.[1] That is commitment that you rarely see from public officials. And let me just point out the fact that he was serving as the mayor of Newark at the time. Could you ever see someone like President Donald Trump running into a burning building to save a human life? Didn't think so.

The senator tends to submerge himself into everything that he does to the fullest extent. He never goes halfway in, and his actions in the Newark fire prove it. Booker is always wholly committed to something that he devotes himself to; he is a "go big or go home" kind of guy. And that's the kind of elected official that the American people deserve: someone who is focused on the job at hand, not focused on making their own wallet thicker.

Booker makes sure that he stays in touch, face-to-face, with the people that he serves in order to represent them to the best of his ability and not lose touch by living in an ivory tower. He proved that in 1998 when he moved into a housing project, where he lived until 2006. He didn't leave the building until he was evicted due to an incoming development. But Booker wouldn't leave without making sure there were some concessions given by the Newark Housing Authority, which, according to the *New York Times*, "promised to build a gentler, kinder Brick Towers to replace the forbidding twin slabs that had become magnets for drugs, violence and despair. The holdouts were also given first dibs in the new quarters."[2]

Even though Booker gets criticized often by press for the fact he has numerous corporate ties via donations to his Senate campaign, it's still clear via his record and his actions that he stands for the working people. His actions show that he's a devoted and honest public servant. And you can tell that he actually cares about the American people, unlike the current administration. He shows love and empathy and commitment to the progressive ideals that can truly make our country better. And he genuinely is concerned about the route of America—so concerned that he's called for Trump's impeachment. Mueller's "statement makes it clear," he said, that "Congress has a legal and moral obligation to begin impeachment proceedings immediately. This administration has continued to stonewall Congress's oversight. Beginning impeachment proceedings is the only path forward."[3] This makes Booker one of the most vocal senators in opposition to Donald Trump, which will play well in the Democratic primary.

Booker also has strongly stood up to the Republican Party, especially since Trump took over the White House. During the Brett Kavanaugh hearings, you could see Booker's leadership on display. Even though he had the one ill-received gaffe when he made a comment about Spartacus,[4] it's still overwhelmingly clear his actions were powerful, and they helped push back against the Supreme Court nomination.

Booker was on the front line defending women who were accusing Kavanaugh of sexual misconduct. There were not many other men who stepped up and really spoke out for them. It was leadership that Washington desperately needed at the time. Republicans led the way to discredit all of Kavanaugh's accusers, and to make the issue as divisive and seemingly partisan as possible to downplay the seriousness of the charges against

Kavanaugh. But Booker cut through that madness and was one of only a few senators who really helped pave the way for women like Christine Blasey Ford to come forward and speak out. It took guts for Booker to get loud and even risk losing his Senate seat by releasing documents that the Republicans were trying to hide surrounding Kavanaugh's work history.[5]

Booker has many different strengths on top of his personal life experience that position him to be a formidable challenger for the Democratic nomination.

One of those strengths is his effort to remain committed to bipartisanship. Over the years, Booker's proven himself to be a progressive who can reach across the aisle to Republicans. He's been reaching across aisles consistently for years, even in other facets of his life, including religion. He even served as the first non-Jewish president of a Jewish student organization while studying at Oxford University under his Rhodes Scholarship.[6]

Perhaps Booker's most striking positive quality is his contagious charisma, which permeates throughout rooms. He does best when he's one-on-one with people or in small groups. And he truly connects to these voters, especially those that are struggling. He's able to offer up complex solutions in a simple format and in a way that translates easily to the American people. Booker's also able to read the fine print so the people don't get screwed by behind-the-scenes deals. He looks at legislation from all angles while figuring out where all of the loopholes are and who really benefits from them, while digging into the gritty details. Being able to effectively analyze and distill Senate bills with their constituents in mind is an ability very few senators have, and Booker has it to spare. His record shows it, and it will benefit him on the campaign trail.

Another strength for Booker's campaign is the fact he's such a great public speaker. When he talks, he has a great buildup in his volume where he can sometimes speak softly and you could hear a pin drop. He will have captured the room. Then he pulls people in, building up from silence to a loud roar in the crowd.

Booker has a great ability to connect with people based on their experience and what their issues are. He can answer to most campaign issues across the board and has a solution to those issues as well. While the solution to that issue may not be something others agree upon, at least he is well-informed about the issue and is willing to learn more about it. I don't know a bill that he hasn't read, and there are few other senators you could say that about. He's always been a responsible and upstanding senator.

Something else that's a great strength for Booker's campaign is the fact he's smart. And when I say smart, I mean very, very intelligent. Booker was a Rhodes Scholar who went to both Yale Law School and Stanford for undergrad on a football scholarship.

Not only is Booker book-smart, he also doesn't mind getting his hands dirty. What I mean by that is Booker doesn't just learn by studying, he also learns by doing. He isn't afraid to go into the dangerous neighborhoods and figure out how to solve problems in a community by actually being there and seeing things firsthand; he gets opinions from people in the community, instead of just getting them from his staff. He lives the experience instead of just hearing about it from a third party while in Washington, DC, and will be able to rely on examples of him doing just that during debates.

Another thing Booker's got going for him is his wealth of political experience spanning over two decades. In recent years, the American people have really considered inexperience or a fresh face to be a benefit. We've learned the hard way that is not always the case. And with all of Trump's rampant corruption that will need to be uncovered, the next American president should be knowledgeable of how the government works so they can hit the ground running. They should at least know a bill becomes a law, what's in the Constitution or Bill of Rights, and have a solid grasp on what the United States is founded upon. All of that alone is a pretty low bar. But Booker, unlike the current president, has the experience and intelligence to navigate the intricacies of the presidency, and we can feel confident in his legislative understanding and ability.

Another strength for Booker's campaign that can't go unmentioned is his relationship with actress Rosario Dawson. That type of power couple isn't always seen in politics. Dawson even started to join Booker on the campaign trail. She was in the audience for an interview Booker did with RuPaul, which was their first public appearance together.[7] Dawson's assumed endorsement of Booker's run, along with her millions of followers on social media and credibility through her years of activism, all equals an extra boost to Booker's campaign that separates him from the pack.

I thought Booker would be less likely to attack opponents, including Trump, which would make it harder for him to stand out. But recently Booker responded to comments former Vice President Joe Biden made:

> "I was in a caucus with James O. Eastland. He never called me 'boy,' he always called me 'son.'" The former vice president then brought up deceased Georgia Sen. Herman Talmage, "[He was] one of the meanest

guys I ever knew, you go down the list of all these guys. Well, guess what? At least there was some civility. We got things done. We didn't agree on much of anything. We got things done. We got it finished. But today, you look at the other side and you're the enemy. Not the opposition, the enemy. We don't talk to each other anymore."[8]

Booker replied to the comment by saying:

I listened to the full totality of what he was talking about, and, frankly, I heard from many, many African Americans who found the comments hurtful. Look, we make mistakes, we sometimes tread upon issues that maybe we aren't knowledgeable of. I don't think the vice president should need this lesson, but this was a time for him to be healing and to be helpful, especially the time that he is looking to bring this party together and lead us in what is the most important election of our lifetime.[9]

Booker's full-throttle response received a little less merit after Congressman John Lewis replied to the controversy, stating, "I don't think the remarks are offensive. During the height of the civil rights movement we worked with people and got to know people that were members of the Klan. . . . We never gave up on our fellow human being."[10] Still, it was powerful to see Booker take such a strong, principled stance on something against another

Democratic candidate. The response seems to be setting the stage for a newer and tougher Booker, the kind of Booker who could take on Trump.

But there are a few negatives surrounding Booker's campaign.

One major concern is the fact Booker has numerous ties to Wall Street, as he's taken in over $2.82 million from the securities and investment industry since 2013.[11] Now, keep in mind his proximity to New York City in Newark. And even though for his presidential campaign Booker is not accepting any contributions from corporate political action committees (PACs),[12] those Wall Street ties could still pose as a major problem with progressives.

As a former Democratic political fund-raiser, I always find it funny when Democratic political candidates made a pledge to not accept PAC money in general, or a specific kind of PAC contribution, whether from labor unions, corporations, or associations. Because in all likelihood in a crowded primary, a lot of those PACs won't be giving anyone money, anyway. They have the excuse of it being too crowded of a field to give. So it's not like candidates like Booker are making a tough commitment, or losing a lot of money over it. The individual money given to the campaign solely due to Booker making that pledge probably raised more for his campaign than corporations would ever give him via their PAC.

And on top of his ties to Wall Street, Booker has strong ties to Facebook's founder Mark Zuckerberg. Booker was able to secure a $100 million donation from Zuckerberg for Newark's school system.[13] With all of the controversy surrounding Facebook and privacy concerns nowadays, this seemingly close tie of Booker's might be something he needs to separate himself from a little further. It is a big concern for progressives if the candidate is tied to Facebook, especially if large sums of money have ever changed hands during a relationship, no matter what the money was for.

People might have some issues with the contributions he's accepted for his campaigns over the years, but it's still hard to view Booker as anything less than a stalwart progressive, with his strong stances on LGBTQ rights, a woman's right to choose, and his solutions to combat gun violence

So when it's all said and done, can Booker win the Democratic primary?

Possibly, but based on his polling in a crowded field, it will take a combination of hard work, luck, and delivering the strongest performance at multiple debates in order to win. It might even take a top candidate dropping out in order for there to be a wide enough of an opening for Booker to push through.

No matter which way you look at it, Booker has a tough path to victory.

He would have to get at least third place in Iowa, and at least third place in New Hampshire, as well. Right now he is polling at seventh place in Iowa[14] and tied for sixth in New Hampshire.[15]

Another roadblock for Booker is the fact he shares so many policy stances with the other candidates. It's hard to say something that someone else is not saying, and it's hard to win over supporters overall when there's twenty-five candidates running for president. At the time of writing, he's not polling very well nationally either, hovering around 2.3 percent, good for seventh place.[16] That, coupled with the fact that Booker has less name recognition than national figures like Joe Biden and Bernie Sanders, makes it all a tougher hill to climb.

Sanders and others have also already figured out what their main campaign messages are. Booker has yet to really define what makes him stand out.

But there is a route for victory. There's a way for Booker to win. His charisma and public speaking skill will serve him well in debates. He's just going to have to do a lot of hard work, meet as many voters as possible, try to snag endorsements before others do, and coming up with a message that hooks people on to his campaign over the others. None of that is easy.

But based on his past of hard work and determination, I wouldn't count Booker out.

Even if he wins the Democratic primary, can he beat Trump? It's clear to me that Booker would mop the floor with Trump. In my opinion, Booker would win in a landslide.

And if he makes it to the White House, rest assured that Booker would make a great president. He would work with all sides on most major issues, and try to come up with a solution that works for everybody. He's able to deal with tough situations in high-stress environments without lashing out like a child to the press or on Twitter. He would serve in the role of president with passion and dignity, and he would bring compassion back into the White House. You'd see a very loving role model in Booker that exemplifies the best of what America has to offer, and be able to see a more progressive shift in our legislation across the country.

You'd never see Booker slacking off or being lazy, and you'd never see Booker commit any corrupt acts like trying to make money from the office. Booker would hire qualified staff that deserve the positions, not just his friends and family. He would make sure that there's diversity within the White House and his cabinet, he'd make a point of restoring ethics in Washington and injecting the truth back into the Oval Office.

America would be lucky to have Cory Booker serve as the next president of the United States—if he can break out of the Democratic field.

WHAT DEFINES CORY BOOKER?

Senator Cory Booker's candidacy rests upon his American dream résumé and down-to-earth common touch, the son of civil rights activists who earned an elite education that he took to New Jersey's gritty largest city where he rose from a tenants' rights lawyer to its mayor and into Congress where he's a major advocate for justice reforms. He declared his presidential campaign on February 1, 2019, without an exploratory committee.

Cory Booker's seven-year record as mayor of Newark is documented in detail due the media-rich environment, less than twenty miles from New York City. He was a celebrity mayor, but his practices over the two terms he served laid a solid foundation for growth in Newark that is still expanding today.

Booker's rise to national fame as a "SuperMayor" was completed after he selflessly ran into a burning building to rescue on of his neighbors, became a national Obama campaign surrogate, and then later in the year opened his doors to Newarkers afflicted by Hurricane Sandy. His term in the Senate began earlier than anyone expected after New Jersey's senior senator passed away in office. But nobody was surprised when he trounced a field of Democratic luminaries to win the office.

Cory Booker is aiming his candidacy squarely at the Obama coalition of progressive voters including voters of color, the religious left, and those who want progressive policies tempered with a leader who has executive experience.

Cory Booker's campaign published its policy agenda in a *Medium* blog that it shares on his widely followed Twitter account, though not on its official website. The New Jersey senator is campaigning on policies of criminal justice reform and resolving income inequality issues that have grown a stark divide between America's mostly working poor and its wealthy leisure class. Lastly, he is very focused on resolving immigration issues by dismantling the federal system that Republicans have commandeered under President Trump and used to create a new mass incarceration of refugees at our southern border, who the federal government forces to live in camps with squalid conditions.

Cory Booker is a Stanford University grad, a Rhodes Scholar, and Yale-trained lawyer who preferred moving to Newark's inner city and fighting his way up the ladder against its machine politics with help from outside donors. He lost his first race for mayor of Newark, which was documented in the Oscar-nominated documentary *Street Fight* that portrayed a crooked incumbent willing to do literally anything to win. But he parlayed that political experience into a victory that landed him in the mayor's office in the next election, at the age of thirty-seven. His adopted hometown of Newark went into decline after the 1967 riots, after which 36 percent of residents left town, but today the city stands as a story of urban revival after Booker's efforts yielded a gusher of cash, development, and two major corporate headquarters that created thousands of jobs. Newark's population began expanding during Mayor Booker's tenure and continues to grow. There are debates about Booker's efficacy as mayor, but there's no doubt that he left the city better than he found it.

On Cory Booker's side is a massive following on social media; he became one of America's first pioneers in using it—Twitter in particular—to help govern a large city. He had over a million followers during his first term of office, and that led to high-profile efforts to burnish the city's public reputation. However, he could face questions about the unseemly behavior of his former subordinates in the city of Newark, some of whom got ensnared in a major criminal case that led to convictions after he joined the Senate. But Booker's overall record is considered one of integrity and he broke the city's infamous four-decade streak of mayors convicted of corruption charges.

In the Senate, Cory Booker has been a leader of the Resistance. If not for the New Jersey senator's activism in early 2017, who knows if the movement opposing President Trump would have taken off like it did.

In the Senate, he's an active sponsor and author of bills, whose biggest accomplishment just passed into law at the end of 2018. The First Step Act is one of many criminal justice reforms that Booker has pressed from his appointment on the Senate judiciary committee. Senator Booker learned a strong lesson about the Trump administration's hatred of immigrants early when he led protests against the Muslim ban, and he's translated that into a legislative program that would change the face of immigration in America. Booker will find support among gun reform activists with his detailed policy agenda to make America safer.

He's not the only former mayor in the race, and his educational résumé and story of urban revival is very similar to the youngest major candidate in the race, South Bend mayor Pete Buttigieg. New York City's mayor is also running for president, though that is not expected to impact Booker's standing, and the New Jersey senator likely has as much name recognition as Bill de Blasio in the Big Apple. Former San Antonio mayor Julián Castro is also in the race; Castro has experience in the Obama administration, where he served as Secretary of Housing and Urban Development.

Senator Booker has a lot to offer to voters in terms of having an inspirational message, while acknowledging the difficult political realities we face, and having a thorough domestic policy vision which he must articulate into an agenda during the campaign. Booker brings experience to the race, both on Main Street and in the Capitol. It remains to be seen if that becomes an enticement to primary voters or a negative. If he doesn't win the primary, there are solid political reasons that he could still land a spot on the bottom of the ticket.

Cory Booker has a tough task ahead to separate from the pack of front-runners into the top tier of candidates, but he's already three-quarters of the way there by consistently polling above 1 percent during the early going of the race before the first Democratic primary debates in Miami, Florida, at the end of June 2019.

NEWARK'S "SUPERMAYOR" BECOMES A HOUSEHOLD NAME

Cory Booker's rise to the national spotlight began with the mayor making an improbable rescue and national headlines, and culminated with his entry into the U.S. Senate. Booker's profile on the national stage ballooned. He trended on Twitter, gave a widely celebrated DNC speech, and, soon after Booker declared his campaign to run for the U.S. Senate, New Jersey's elderly senior senator called it quits. That led to an off-year special election, which he won.

The first time Mayor Booker made the news outside of Newark came early, when he ran for Newark's top job, and continued later when a documentary about his first mayoral campaign came out and got nominated for an Oscar. As mayor, he had an outsized national profile for implementing First Lady Michelle Obama's youth fitness program and landing a major investment from Facebook founder and CEO Mark Zuckerberg. His dogged promotion of Newark and his humble displays of public service had already kept him intermittently in the national news spotlight for many years before April 12, 2012.

What happened next turned him into a household name in America.

It all started late on a typical Tuesday night, when the mayor arrived at his home after a local television interview, according to the *Star-Ledger*.[1] Booker saw flames pouring out of a two-story building next door and rushed into the burning building. After getting the rest of the family out of the home's lower floor, Booker, against his security detail's advice for his own safety, rushed up to the second floor to find the family's grown daughter. She was trapped and crying for help as the flames rose and the man who started the kitchen fire was still trying to put it out.

Suddenly Booker realized that he might be trapped in the burning structure when he had a hard time finding her on the second floor. He even contemplated having to take a flying leap out of the upstairs window to escape the flames. But he found the girl when she cried out from a back bedroom and quickly "grabbed her and whipped her out of bed." He went downstairs through the burning kitchen with forty-seven-year-old Zina Hodges slung over his shoulder, and both collapsed.[2] Medics arrived to treat Mayor Booker for second-degree burns on his hand and the woman for smoke inhalation. Mayor Booker's rescue made global headlines.

"Thanks 2 all who are concerned," he tweeted shortly after escaping the inferno.[3] "Just suffering smoke inhalation. We got the woman out of the house. We are both off to hospital. I will b ok." The next morning, Twitter erupted over the rescue with the humorous satirical hashtag #CoryBookerStories trending nationally. Booker tweeted that it "brought him smiles" as people jokingly compared him to Superman.[4]

The mayor was discharged from the hospital at 6 a.m. the following morning and appeared on *CBS This Morning*, where he called it a "come to Jesus" moment. He held a press conference a few hours later, with his hand bandaged from the burns. But Booker dismissed the nickname "superhero," and calling himself just "a neighbor that did what most neighbors would do."

Until that day, Cory Booker's mayorship was regionally important in the country's largest media market. After that day, his rise to national prominence became inexorable, but it wasn't a straight line.

A month after the big rescue, Mayor Booker made a humorous video entitled "Don't worry, we've got this" with Republican then-vice presidential hopeful, New Jersey Governor Chris Christie (R).[5] During the course of the three-minute video, Booker satirically upstages Christie to save the day, anywhere from fixing a flat tire to catching a falling baby (doll) in the Capitol. It ended with the mayor "taking" a call from then-presumptive Republican presidential nominee Mitt Romney in the governor's office and pretending to turn down the VP nomination by saying, "I'm not a number two guy, I'm not a background singer. . . ."

It was a bipartisan hit.

President Obama's campaign made Booker a high-profile surrogate soon after the big rescue, which led to a prime-time speech at the Democratic National Committee. Between those two events, Booker made comments on NBC's long-running Sunday morning show *Meet the Press* that led to a media firestorm because of his strong, telling comments slamming negative campaigning. *Politico* reports:

> *Newark Mayor Cory Booker, a rising Democratic star, criticized on Sunday the Obama campaign's attack ad against Mitt Romney for his work at Bain Capital. "It's*

nauseating to the American public," Booker said on NBC's Meet the Press. "Enough is enough. Stop attacking private equity. Stop attacking Jeremiah Wright."

"As far as that stuff, I have to just say from a very personal level I'm not about to sit here and indict private equity," he added. "To me, it's just we're getting to a ridiculous point in America. Especially that I know I live in a state where pension funds, unions and other people invest in companies like Bain Capital. If you look at the totality of Bain Capital's record, they've done a lot to support businesses [and] to grow businesses. And this, to me, I'm very uncomfortable with."[6]

Cory Booker's donors on Wall Street cheered the move, but President Obama's supporters cringed as the surrogate attacked the campaign he was supposed to be representing. The mayor had raised nearly a quarter of the multimillion-dollar 2002 war chest directly from Manhattan financiers, and it was no secret he had his eyes on a 2014 Senate campaign.[7] Obama was fiercely critical of Wall Street's central role in the Great Recession of 2008, though he didn't seek to prosecute an avalanche of fraudulent financial dealings while in office. But regardless, the president's campaign spent a significant amount of time shining a light on now-Senator Mitt Romney's time at the private equity firm Bain Capital, much of which centered on laying off Americans to outsource jobs to foreign countries.

"The Booker calculation, in other words, is probably that the average Democratic voter's memory of his outburst will fade long before

2014—but that the average Wall Street donor's won't," wrote MSNBC's current election map specialist Steve Kornacki in a column for *Salon*.[8] "[A]nyone who's followed the enormously ambitious Newark mayor's career closely knows he's not one to pull a Joe Biden. He's just too smart and too smooth to screw up so epically. More likely, Booker went on the show to help himself and to advance his own long-term political prospects. And on that score, his appearance was a success."

Most columnists noted that at the time that it was no secret that Cory Booker had his eyes on the Senate, and the ailing eighty-eight year old incumbent Democrat Frank Lautenberg faced reelection in 2014. Speculation was also running rampant that Booker might take on Gov. Christie in 2013, whose political star as a "red" governor in a "blue state" was still rising back then, before the BridgeGate scandal made him the least popular governor in America by 2017.

The mayor released a YouTube video that evening in which he "walked his comments back" in the euphemistic parlance of the political class, which happens when a politician says what they really mean but the comment upsets someone. In it, he admitted that Romney's record at Bain is fair game because he involved it in his political campaign.[9] The mayor continued to raise money for the president, but didn't make any further media appearances that summer.

Three months later, Booker told the *Wall Street Journal* that it was "dumb decision to do the hostage video" recanting his comments, but that President Obama told him it was "small potatoes."[10] He has since deleted the video from YouTube.

However, the surrogate mess did not stop Mayor Booker from being invited to that September's Democratic National Convention in Charlotte, North Carolina, on its first night. The party asked him to present its platform to the convention for a formal vote, and in just ten minutes his speech roused the crowd and demonstrated his Democratic bona fides to a national audience. Booker's speech kicked off the gathering with a standing ovation.

"It's not about left or right but about moving America and our economy forward. Our platform and our president stands firm in the conviction that America must continue to out-build, out-innovate, and out-educate the world," began Booker to a smattering of applause.[13] "You see, this platform is a clear choice between economic pathways, forward or back, inclusion or exclusion, grow together as a nation or be a country of savage disparities that favor the fortunate few over the greatest driving force of any economy, a large and robust middle class." He continued:

We must choose forward. We must choose inclusion. We must choose growing together. We choose American might and American muscle, standing strong on the bedrock of the American ideal, a strong and empowered, an ever-expanding and ever-growing middle class.

Our platform emphasizes that a vibrant, free, and fair market is essential to economic growth. We also must pull from our highest ideals of justice and fairness to protect against those ills that destabilized our economy in recent years, like predatory lending, overleveraged financial institutions, and the unchecked avarice of the past that trumped fairness and common sense. Our platform calls for significant cuts in federal spending. Our platform calls for a balanced deficit reduction plan, where everyone, everyone, from elected officials to the wealthy and the super wealthy, pay their fair share.

And please listen to this, because when your country is in a costly war, with our soldiers sacrificing abroad and our nation is facing a debt crisis at home, being asked to pay your fair share isn't class warfare—it's patriotism.

Before he could continue, the room erupted in loud applause and the gathered Democratic delegates broke into a spontaneous chant of "U-S-A., U-S-A." Given the big stage, Cory Booker didn't disappoint. Little did he know that his role in the 2012 presidential campaign wasn't over that night, and that what happened next in his home state of New Jersey would land front and center just eight short weeks later.

Superstorm Sandy landed eight days before election day 2012, devastating the state of New Jersey.[14] Thirty-seven people in New Jersey lost their lives. The state suffered over thirty billion dollars' worth of property damage. Newark got walloped with hurricane-strength winds, and most of its residents became part of the group of 1.7 million residents who lost power.

Mayor Booker leapt into action, using Twitter to post around a hundred times per day to help his constituents cope with losing power in the storm. "In the past few days, Booker made an especially personal gesture when he invited neighbors over to his house to relax, charge their cell phones and watch movies," wrote *Time* magazine about the mayor's generous gesture to his neighbors. "When about 12 Newark citizens took Booker up on his offer, he tweeted to let them know that they could request DVDs and that he was having lunch delivered."

"I don't have faith in many politicians," tweeted Newark resident Michael Phillips.[15] "But I have faith in Mayor @CoryBooker of Newark. A true warrior for his constituents. #Sandy." From getting trees off buildings to delivering food, water, and baby supplies, it seemed that maybe the satirical video he filmed with Gov. Christie was true. Mayor Booker seemed to be everywhere people were in need, all at once. One Newark resident asked him for help because he ran out of Hot Pockets; "Cory Booker Finally Solves Newark's Hot Pockets Crisis" blared *Time's* tongue-in-cheek but true headline after the company sent residents a blizzard of coupons after the tweet went viral.[16]

President Obama spoke with Gov. Christie, who asked him to visit New Jersey in the aftermath of the storm, dropping politics in the face of a massive natural disaster.[17] When the two men shared a warm handshake—caught on camera—and the Republican governor praised Obama effusively, members of his own party went wild.[18] The *New York Times* even speculated that Christie was so warm with Obama just because he wanted to fend off a challenge from Cory Booker.[19]

What they didn't know is that the president had actually given Christie his direct phone number, and put the full resources of the federal government at his disposal.[20] (President Obama also healed the rift between Christie and legendary rock star Bruce Springsteen.[21]) Mayor Booker explained the real source of unexpected comity during the heat of the last week of a presidential campaign to *Politico*:

> *"Let's call it as it is," Booker said. "President Obama has been really hands-on in this. The governor's heard from him numerous times, I've been on calls with him numerous times. He's taking a personal interest. . . . He's been doing an incredible job cutting through red tape, connecting directly with those affected."*
>
> *Booker, an Obama surrogate, has long been considered a top contender to face off with Christie in New Jersey's 2013 gubernatorial race—but he wasn't looking to talk politics Wednesday morning. "This isn't politics," Booker said. "Right now it's just human beings facing human tragedy and pulling together to do so."*[22]

The end result of the bipartisan partnership to help New Jersey was over 1.5 million meals and 1.6 million liters of water delivered and over $5.6 billion in cash aid distributed in the state only twelve months after the storm.[23] Over a thousand New Jerseyans remain displaced because of the storm as of April 2019, and the state is still expanding its recovery programs seven years later.[24] Nobody can really say if the president's response to Sandy swung the 2012 election, but Obama won reelection by a solid margin on November 6, 2012.

Nearly a month after the election, another one of Booker's Twitter discussions led him to something that began attracting attention to his political career in Washington, DC. He decided to take the "SNAP Challenge," and to live on the same $30 weekly budget that an economically disadvantaged person on government food assistance might use to eat.[25] It was an act of humility and caffeine withdrawal to learn firsthand the effects of hunger on the impoverished, and when he burned his baked sweet potato, Booker learned firsthand what it's like when you make a cooking mistake and you can't afford to throw out the results.[26]

Four days before the Christmas holiday, Cory Booker declared his intention to explore a run for Sen. Lautenberg's seat in 2014 with a column in the *Star-Ledger*:

> *This is a significant moment in our nation's history for Newark, cities like it, and for all Americans. We must confront a catastrophic debt crisis that could devastate the middle class, find ways to empower hard-working low income Americans, bring urgency to the effort to educate all our children, reform a broken immigration system, deliver marriage equality to all Americans, and bring sanity to our national gun safety laws.*
>
> *These are the hard won lessons I have learned in Newark: if you can bring people together around common ideals, if you can inspire people to see the universal truth that we are all in this together, that we need each other, that our destinies are interwoven, then great things can happen. I have seen how you can ignite in people the spirit of our ancestors; the spirit of service and sacrifice*

and of the dignity of hard work for families and for higher
principles. When you do that great things do happen, and
miracles are made manifest. This is the story of Newark's
enduring spirit and the reason for our progress in recent
years.[27]

Two months after later, Sen. Lautenberg announced that he would not run for reelection in 2014, but he didn't finish his term, and before 2013 ended Cory Booker would go on to join the United States Senate after a trying special election.[28]

While Mayor Booker's reputation was widely known in political circles before the events of 2012, his amazing rescue and subsequent events directly led to his elevation to the Senate, the office which defines his political career to this day.[29]

CAMPAIGN PLATFORM

Senator Cory Booker has not published a campaign issues website page or created a policy agenda as of late June 2019. But he has submitted bills to Congress that tell a story about his policy preferences, and his official campaign *Medium* posts build on those plans. He has not fleshed out a detailed foreign policy position, paper, or speech as of the week of the first 2020 Democratic primary debate.

Booker's top initiatives are criminal justice reform, commonsense gun reforms, a pilot program for a federal jobs guarantee, and special savings plan, known as "baby bonds," which is intended to combat wealth inequality. He cosponsored a Senate resolution backing Rep. Alexandria Ocasio-Cortez's (D-NY) Green New Deal and believes in treating health care as a right, along with a "Medicare for All" plan for universal insurance coverage.

Senator Booker's liberal ideology is very much in line with the mainstream of Democratic Party thinking in New Jersey, a solidly Democratic-leaning state with a lot of residents involved in Wall Street finance and Big Pharma. Booker wants to extend the social safety net to promote a better life for regular people who earn less, but his progressive policies are tempered by a pro-business bent that his benefactors appreciate. Booker wants to institute new laws to expand gun background checks, and has sponsored assault weapons ban legislation. Senator Booker is a dogged advocate for criminal justice reform and wants to reform immigration with an ambitious piece of legislation aimed at reversing the system detaining asylum seekers.

The senator's early campaign is heavily based around his personal narrative, his aspirational rhetoric, and his consistent progressive political leanings accompanied by a prolific flurry of legislative proposals. (The issues presented below are listed in no specific order of importance.)

HEALTH CARE

Senator Booker supports "Medicare for All" as put forward by Sen. Sanders.[1] The senator came out in favor of Medicare for all in September 2017, when he published an article on *Medium* describing his discussion with civil rights legend Congressman John Lewis (GA-D), which noted how Lewis was denied health care after being injured during a 1965 voting rights march in Selma, Alabama.[2] "Health care should be an American right," said Booker, "not a mark of economic status out of reach to many just because they don't make enough money."

"The US spends more on healthcare per person than any other country in the world, yet we report worse health outcomes than our peer nations," he recently wrote to his 4.6 million Twitter followers.[3] "Medicare for All is the best way to ensure that every American has access to quality, affordable health care." He will have to explain past votes against drug reimportation in the context of donations from the pharmaceutical industry, which has numerous businesses in his home state.[4] In January 2019, he joined Senator

Richard Blumenthal (D-CT) and Senator Bernie Sanders (D-VT) in cosponsoring a bill to lower drug prices with three major subsections:

- The Prescription Drug Price Relief Act, which would peg the price of prescription drugs in the United States to the median price in five major countries: Canada, the United Kingdom, France, Germany, and Japan;
- The Medicare Drug Price Negotiation Act, which would direct the Secretary of Health and Human Services (HHS) to negotiate lower prices for prescription drugs under Medicare Part D;
- The Affordable and Safe Prescription Drug Importation Act, which would allow patients, pharmacists, and wholesalers to import safe, affordable medicine from Canada and other major countries. This bill was originally introduced by Senators Booker, Sanders, and Bob Casey (D-PA) in 2017.[5]

"There is no reason that, in a country as rich as ours, Americans should be choosing between paying for prescription drugs and paying for food and other necessities," Booker said when releasing the bill. "And incredibly, despite an enormous tax windfall from the Trump tax cuts, drug manufacturers aren't lowering prices—they're issuing stock buybacks to their shareholders and in many cases raising prices."

DEVELOPING A FEDERAL JOBS GUARANTEE

One of Senator Booker's signature issues is creating a program to allow all citizens who want to work in a series of test communities the opportunity to do so, with the intent of expanding the program nationally. The Federal Jobs Guarantee Development Act would create a three-year pilot program to target up to fifteen high-unemployment communities and regions across America.

"There is great dignity in work—and in America, if you want to provide for your family, you should be able to find a full-time job that pays a fair wage," Senator Booker said in the bill's announcement in April 2018.[6] "Both Martin Luther King, Jr. and President Franklin Roosevelt believed that every American had the right to a job, and that right has only become more important in this age of increasing income inequality, labor market concentration, and continued employment discrimination."

If passed, every adult in the pilot communities would be guaranteed a job with a minimum wage phasing up to $15 per hour with health benefits and paid family and sick leave. It would also expand the Work Opportunity Tax Credit to incentivize private employers to hire those in the guaranteed jobs program.

Senator Booker's bipartisan Fair Chance Act, also known as the "Ban the box" Act—which Rep. Elijah Cummings (D-MA) introduced in the House—was unanimously voted out of the House judiciary committee in March 2019 with sponsorship from that panel's ranking member, Rep. Doug Collins (R-GA). The act was advanced out of committee in the Senate as well, and as of June 2019 was awaiting a final vote in both chambers of Congress.[7]

"This bipartisan bill will break down the barriers that prevent people who have paid their debt to society from getting a job," wrote the senator when the bill was released, "so that we can better advance our goals of justice, rehabilitation, and redemption for all. 'Banning the box' would mean that initial job applications would not ask prospective employees if they've been convicted of a crime, as a means of ensuring that people who've been rehabilitated by the criminal justice system get decent opportunities to get a job and therefore have a better chance of re-entering society."[8]

BOOKER'S "BABY BONDS" PROGRAM

One of Senator Booker's top priorities is addressing America's chronic problem with income inequality. His American Opportunity Accounts Act seeks to mitigate the wealth gap by creating a savings account for every child in America when they're born. Each year, funds would be added depending on the parents' income, and the cash would accrue interest until the child turns eighteen years old and can access the fund. Booker plans to pay for the program by reforming the estate tax on the very wealthiest Americans and rolling back the Trump tax cuts to the wealthy and restoring income tax rates to 2009 levels.

"Today, nearly one in three American families have zero to negative wealth, and it's hard to get ahead if you begin life behind the starting line," said the senator when he released the new bill in October 2018.[9] "Everyone in America should have a real shot to succeed, but federal policy over decades and an upside down tax code that heaps benefits on the very rich and big corporations have grown the gap between those who have much and those who have little."

The way the plan would work would be to deposit one thousand dollars as seed money when the baby is born, then up to an additional two thousand dollars annually, depending on family income. The money would sit in a federally insured account managed by the U.S. Treasury department, which would achieve roughly a 3 percent interest rate. For families living below the poverty line, the child's benefit when withdrawn at eighteen years old would be an estimated $46,215, according to the senator's office. Children whose parents earn $125,751 (roughly five times the poverty line) or more would receive a benefit of $1,681, and kids whose families earn the median income in America would get a benefit of nearly thirteen thousand dollars.

Booker also supports a $15/hour minimum wage to combat inequality and end "poverty wages" for the working poor.[10] He's proposed a bill expanding the Earned Income Tax Credit (EITC), a payment from the government to working poor people though the tax system, whether they have to pay taxes themselves or not.[11] The senator's "Rise Credit" proposal is similar broad strokes to his opponent Sen. Kamala Harris's (D-CA) plan to expand the credit in such a way that it nearly becomes a basic income program. Booker wouldn't include caregivers and other nontraditional work categories in his plan, but it would double the income threshold for receiving the EITC and multiply times eight the amount that a single worker who gets the credit can earn. Senator Booker would raise the maximum payout by 25 percent to $650 a month for a working married couple.

Alongside House Whip James Clyburn (D-SC), the New Jersey senator sponsored a bill in October 2018 to expand the anti-poverty funding formula called 10-20-30, which directs whichever federal account targeted to deliver 10 percent of its funding to communities with a poverty level of 20 percent over the last thirty years.[12]

FIGHTING GUN VIOLENCE

Cory Booker's platform on gun control is heavily influenced by his seven-year tenure as mayor of New Jersey's largest city. Senator Booker's plans for the 2020 Democratic primary are outlined in a series of legislative acts.

In the wake of the Las Vegas massacre, the senator joined with his colleague Senator Menendez to introduce a series of commonsense gun laws in the Automatic Gunfire Prevention Act.[13] It would ban bump stocks—a move that even the Trump administration later chose to undertake through an executive order after the NRA lobbied congressional Republicans not to support legislation—and close a major gun sale loophole allowing people who would otherwise not be allowed to buy a gun to legally purchase a weapon.

"Fully automatic firearms have no place in our society. We must ban devices that can convert semi-automatic rifles into fully automatic weapons," the senator said in a press release. "Another common sense step is to make sure that people who would fail a background check aren't able to exploit a loophole to get a gun."

A month later, Booker introduced an assault weapons ban that would end the sale of any weapon that accepts a detachable ammunition magazine and has military characteristics. It would grandfather in present guns and exempt by name over two thousand weapons used for defense or recreational purposes, but require universal background checks, secure safety locks or gun storage for grandfathered weapons, and prohibit high-capacity ammunition magazines from being transferred.[14] Both senators from New Jersey joined to reintroduce a clean bill requiring universal gun background checks in early 2019.[15]

His *Medium* post calls for expanding the Consumer Product Safety Commission's jurisdiction to oversee the gun industry and for repealing legal liability immunity that his 2020 primary opponent Senator Bernie Sanders (D-VT) voted in favor of over a decade ago while serving in the House.[16] Booker would require microstamping on ammunition to help law enforcement solve homicides, closing the "boyfriend loophole" that allows people who shouldn't have guns to use spouses as straw buyers, begin dedicated research on the public health crisis brought on by lax gun laws in America, and modernize the federal Bureau of Alcohol, Tobacco & Firearms (ATF).

Lastly, he would require gun owners to report thefts, create a national "red flags" law to disarm those who imminently threaten murderous violence, and call on the IRS to review the National Rifle Association's tax status as a charity. Predictably, the NRA's lobbying calls Senator Booker's platform "dangerous."[17]

Lastly, Cory Booker considers the above plans part of a separate initiative to prevent firearm suicide. For reference, Australia reduced its gun suicide rate by anywhere from 63 to 74 percent over a twenty-year period after a conservative prime minister oversaw a major gun reform effort in the late 1990s in the wake of a horrifying mass murder.[18]

"Every year in America, nearly 22,000 Americans die by firearm suicide—an average of 59 deaths each day," notes Booker's *Medium* page.

"Veterans are particularly impacted, with more than 6,000 veteran suicides each year—nearly 70 percent of which resulted from firearm injury."[19] These are specific initiatives that New Jersey's junior senator would implement to curb suicides which aren't listed above:

- Implementing a federal licensing program.
- Supporting "lethal means safety counseling."
- Appointing a federal coordinator to cut suicide rate.

There is no single federal official currently in charge of coping with America's rising suicide epidemic, while it has become the tenth-leading cause of death nationally. Booker's plan would use the White House to coordinate efforts to reduce preventable suicides across federal agencies and different levels of government for the very first time.

CRIMINAL JUSTICE REFORM

Cory Booker's commitment to criminal justice reform led to his top achievement in the Senate at the end of 2018. According to his *Medium* page, the Next Step Act is meant to "make serious and substantial reforms to sentencing guidelines, prison conditions, law enforcement practices and training, and reentry efforts for people who are incarcerated." In addition, it would:

- Provide better training for law enforcement officers on implicit racial bias, de-escalation, and use of force.

- Prohibit racial and religious profiling and improve the reporting of police use-of-force incidents.
- Eliminate the racially targeted sentencing disparity between crack and powder cocaine sentences by reducing it from 18:1 to 1:1.
- Reduce harsh mandatory minimums for nonviolent drug offenses.
- End the federal prohibition on marijuana and automatically expunge the records of those convicted on charges of marijuana use and possession.
- Reinvest in the communities most impacted by the failed War on Drugs.
- Improve the ability of those behind bars to stay in touch with their loved ones—which has a proven effect on reducing the risk of recidivism.
- Remove the ban on public assistance and federal Temporary Assistance for Needy Families (TANF) and Supplemental Nutrition Assistance Program (SNAP) benefits for formerly incarcerated nonviolent drug offenders.
- Remove the barriers for people with criminal convictions to receiving an occupational license for jobs, such as hairdressers and taxi drivers.
- Reinstate the right to vote in federal elections for formerly incarcerated individuals.
- "Ban the box"—prohibit federal employers and contractors from asking a job applicant about their criminal history until the final stages of the interview process.

- Create a federal pathway to sealing the records of nonviolent drug offenses for adults and automatically sealing (and in some cases expunging) juvenile records.[20]

That's not all that Cory Booker would do to reform criminal justice if he were elected president. The senator from New Jersey has a separate *Medium* page for his Restoring Justice Initiative, which would use executive clemency "to issue communications for broad classes of individuals currently serving sentences for nonviolent drug offenses widely viewed as unduly harsh and rooted in racist and misguided federal policy."[21]

Explaining that almost half of the federal prison population is made up of drug offenders, he writes that in 2015 America spent $3.3 billion dollars just on those prisoners, and that "We need to change that." Who would benefit from the plan? There are three primary categories of offenders:

- Individuals serving sentences for marijuana-related offenses.
- Individuals serving sentences that would have been reduced under the First Step Act, if all the bill's sentencing provisions had been applied retroactively.
- Individuals currently incarcerated with unjust sentences due to the sentencing disparity between crack and powder cocaine.

Booker would also establish a bipartisan Executive Clemency Panel in the White House to make the process more efficient and order it to give special presumption for those who are above the age of fifty and have already served lengthy sentences, because "evidence suggests that people typically age out of crime and are far less likely to recidivate."

The senator also supports the Justice for the Victims of Lynching Act put forward by his 2020 primary opponent Senator Kamala Harris (D-CA), which would make the despicable acts of public murder that were a hallmark of the Jim Crow era into a federal hate crime.[22]

Lastly, Cory Booker re-introduced the Marijuana Justice Act in the Senate in February 2019, which would legalize weed nationally—which has the support of nearly the entire Democratic primary field—and expunge drug possession crimes linked to the plant.[23] It's the capstone plan of one of Booker's signature Senate initiatives which started when he was just a freshman legislator facing reelection after only a few months on the job, when national opinion wasn't as pro-marijuana as it has become today, with over half the states legalizing or decriminalizing the drug as of mid-2019.

THE REPARATIONS COMMITTEE ACT

Senator Booker released a bill to make a committee to study the federal government paying reparations to the descendants of slavery on April 8, 2019 as a companion bill to Rep. Sheila Jackson-Lee's (D-TX) bill in the House.[24] It would create a commission to study the impact of slavery and the state of racial discrimination in America today. The topic of reparations has become one of the most discussed early issues of the 2020 Democratic primary. In just two months, Booker attracted twelve Senate cosponsors for the bill.[25]

WOMEN'S ISSUES

Senator Booker has three ideas that he'd like to get through Congress if he's elected president, but he knows as well as anyone the difficulty of getting women's rights legislation passed. So he's written a *Medium* post outlining how he'd use the power of the executive to advance a women's right to control her own body, instead of the Republican agenda to let government call the shots.[26] He wrote what he'd do from "day one" in the Oval Office:

- Create a White House Office of Reproductive Freedom.
- End the "domestic gag rule" and expand and modernize the Title X Family Planning Program.
- Guarantee access to employer-covered contraceptive care.
- Repeal the Hyde Amendment in his first presidential budget.

In addition, the senator promises to use the power of judicial appointments to choose judges committed to uphold reproductive rights. Lastly, he supports legislation to codify the landmark Supreme Court ruling *Roe v. Wade*, which would have the effect of preempting the patchwork of state laws aimed at restricting a woman's right to choose.

FOREIGN POLICY

Cory Booker has not made a major foreign policy speech, nor issued a policy position paper or a *Medium* post about how he would change international relations between America and the world. It's safe to say that his views are well within the mainstream of the Democratic Party.

Senator Booker joined the Senate Foreign Affairs Committee in 2017, sitting alongside his fellow New Jersey senator, ranking member Bob Menendez. Three examples of his foreign policy moves in the Senate include:

- Specific to legislation, Sen. Booker sponsored S. Res. 286, which is a resolution to support the role of United States foreign aid to ensure access to education for children in some of the most poverty-stricken countries through the Global Partnership for Education.
- Sen. Booker also personally sponsored S. Res. 616, which is a resolution encouraging the government of Kenya to respect human and civil rights and promote a democratic system of government with open, honest elections and policies. Particularly, this resolution requested that President Kenyatta of Kenya "ensure that extrajudicial killings and other violations are investigated and prosecuted by an independent judicial inquiry."
- Sen. Booker cosponsored a bill that has become law, S. 368, otherwise known as the Global Health Empowerment and Rights Act, which is meant to prohibit application restrictions. It is designed to make eligibility requirements for foreign aid less restrictive so that applications will not be deemed ineligible "solely on the basis of health or medical services."

One of his key positions was backing President Obama's Iran deal—despite heavy lobbying in opposition, sometimes from close friends—which froze the nation's nuclear program for ten years, in exchange for sanctions relief.[27] He had previously cosponsored a bill from Sen. Menendez tightening sanctions on Iran for pursuing enriched uranium that could be used later in a bomb.[28]

AFFORDABLE HOUSING

Senator Cory Booker's personal story about race in America intersected with housing very early on, when his parents had trouble finding a home in New Jersey because of discriminatory housing practices.

Booker introduced a plan on *Medium* in June 2019 that would include a rental credit program to help cap costs of living at 30 percent of income for working-class and middle-class Americans.[29] 57 million Americans could benefit from such a bill. Senator Booker notes that over $200 billion is spent subsidizing homeownership annually through the mortgage interest tax deduction.

One could best describe his housing plan as picking and choosing from his opponents' previously released material, but unlike Senator Elizabeth Warren's (D-MA) plans, he doesn't say how he would pay for the proposal. Booker's proposition is not dissimilar from Sen. Harris's plans to assist renters. But is different than Warren's plan, which primarily uses existing affordable housing trust funds to spur two million new housing units, lowering rents (which tend to rise with inflation) by up to 10 percent over ten years, according to independent expert analysis. However, Booker pledges to give $40 billion annually to those same funds.

The New Jersey senator would also incentivize cities and towns to roll back restrictive zoning regulations—prevalent in his home state—that limit growth and drive up the cost of housing. He'd do that by requiring that more than $16 billion of current funding for a variety of programs gets tied to local governments demonstrating that they're reducing barriers to affordable housing. He would also propose protection from housing discrimination for all Americans, including discrimination based on gender or sexual orientation, and a right to counsel for those facing eviction. Lastly, he would fight to eliminate homelessness with a combination of grants and making the U.S. Interagency Council on Homelessness a permanent body.

IMMIGRATION

Senator Cory Booker has been one of the leaders in fighting the Trump administration's punitive measures against immigrants and asylum seekers, which turned him into an early leader of the resistance, as we explore in chapter 9. But he has backed those speeches up with actions by introducing legislation aimed at curbing the Trump administration's abuses and break up the twenty-year-long expansion of the detention system run by U.S. Immigration and Customs Enforcement's (ICE).[30]

That's why Booker reintroduced the Dignity for Detained Immigrants Act in April 2019. It would end the attorney general's unlimited power to determine who is imprisoned and who is released pending civil immigration hearings. "The Trump administration has adopted the motto of cruelty for cruelty's sake and continues to close America's doors to asylum seekers in their time of need," Booker wrote in a *Medium* post.[31] "The fact that Barr wants to strip asylum seekers of their right to due process violates our Constitution and our country's values. Our bill will hold the Department of Homeland Security accountable and ensures vulnerable immigrants are treated with the dignity and respect that should be expected in this country." He tweeted:

"*Stripping asylum seekers of their right to due process is:*

- *Racist*
- *Inhumane*
- *Unconstitutional*

Take your pick. Either way, it's wrong and we need to end it."[32]

Booker's act would radically reverse the last major immigration bill—passed in 1996—by restricting ICE or the Border Patrol from arresting most immigrants without a warrant signed by an immigration judge. Unlike today, the detained immigrant would be given a mandatory bond hearing within forty-eight hours. It would allow detainees a path to challenge their confinement with a judicial presumption in favor of releasing the immigrant pending any hearings unless there's clear and convincing evidence that they'd be a safety or flight risk. It would raise the standard of detention even higher for crime victims and those with claims to asylum. Family separation would be practically abolished. It would even make judges use a means test to determine the amount of cash bond required to be released, which right now is a minimum of $2,000, which has resulted in $200 million changing hands from immigrants to the federal government, much of which they'll never see again.

He's the only 2020 Democratic nominee, except for former San Antonio mayor Julián Castro, to release a complete immigration plan.

Senator Booker also supports the Dreamer Confidentiality Act, which would safeguard the information of Americans protected under the Deferred Action for Childhood Arrivals (DACA) program.[33] Because the DACA application basically admits that the applicant is undocumented, there is a constant concern that the information could be used in a Republican Party political purge and mass deportation.

FIGHTING AMERICA'S TEACHER SHORTAGE

In February 2018, Senator Booker released the STRIVE Act with two House cosponsors from his home state. The bill would address America's shortage of qualified teachers and give immediate relief to thousands of educators who chose the profession believing that their student loans would be forgiven:

- Increase the teacher tax credit to better reflect how much of their own money teachers invest in educating our students.
- Overhaul the current loan forgiveness program for teachers to provide incremental and complete loan forgiveness to teachers who teach for seven years and grandfathers in those teachers who have taught for longer and are still paying student loans.

- Mandatorily fund and increase funding for programs that pre- pare and train educators to be their most effective, while allowing early childhood educators to participate in the program.
- Encourage diversity in the teaching profession by providing financial assistance for teaching certification and licensing fees to low-income and other underrepresented communities.[34]

A coalition of teacher advocacy groups has endorsed the bill. The necessity for this reform only later became quantified when news reports showed that the Trump administration's Department of Education rejects nearly all requests for student loan forgiveness.[35]

Finally, Booker is famously a practicing vegan, and accordingly he has a top grade on animal-rights issues from the Humane Society.[36]

BIOGRAPHY: FORMATIVE BACKGROUND AND EDUCATION

Cory Anthony Booker's road to presidential politics began on April 27, 1969, in the city of Washington, DC, when he was born to trailblazing parents who were active in the 1960s civil rights movement. His father, Cary Booker, was born in the segregated South to a mother who couldn't care for him, and he was adopted out, before getting an education and becoming one of IBM's first African American executives. His mother, Carolyn Rose Booker (née Jordan), was also an executive at IBM. The small family moved to Bergen County, New Jersey, when Cory was only four months old, struggling to find housing because of their race, before settling down in the suburb of Harrington Park.[1]

While most people do not associate progressive politicians with religion, Senator Booker's faith, and particularly his ecumenical studies, are a central pillar of him as a man and a political actor. Young Cory Booker was raised to learn about his parents' struggles, and they raised him in a religious home that was close to the local African Methodist Episcopal (AME) church.[2] He told *US News & World Report* that the theology he learned in those formative years "helped frame this idea of social justice for me and this idea of a struggle." Booker continued:

> *These are the themes in life which are consistent in Judaism, Islam, Hinduism—of being grounded in who you are and being engaged in an unjust world. Judaism specifically believes that the messiah is just not going to come and save people. Every generation has the opportunity to bring about the messiah by engaging in the world. And black theology is always about the struggle for justice. So seeing that concurrent theme has enriched my love of God and others and has inspired me to live as consistently as possible. So from Gandhi, who is Hindu, to Martin Luther King, who is Christian, to everybody who marched in the civil rights movement—everybody from Jews to blacks to whites to Catholics—they were engaged in a fight, demanding from God. And I may end this world defeated in my goals, I may lose, but that's the righteous path. My frustration with religion is people who think it's about four walls: You go in and are righteous and leave church and it doesn't go with you. I love the great theologian who said, "Everywhere I go I preach the gospel, but only sometimes do I use words." Or, "Before you tell me about your religion, show me how you treat other people."[3]*

In 1987, Cory Booker graduated from Northern Valley Regional High School as a blue-chip recruit in football, despite not having even played competitively as a freshman. Booker was named the Gatorade New Jersey Football Player of the Year and made the *USA Today* All-USA high school team as a defensive back.[4] Top football programs like Michigan and Notre Dame tried to recruit Booker.

"I'll never forget that that year, *U.S. News & World Report* academically ranked the colleges and they ranked Stanford over Harvard and Yale as the number one academic school in the country," Booker told *USA Today* in late 2018, sharing his life plan at that early age.[5] "That sealed it for me. I was like, 'If I have a chance to get a football scholarship to the top academic school, I'm going to take that opportunity,' because even back then, I realized that football was going to be my ticket and not my destination."

Booker had one breakout game in 1990, a four-catch effort in Stanford's Cinderella-story upset of then top-ranked Notre Dame. But the future senator largely played special teams, and had a tough time getting on the field for offensive snaps. He graduated with a Bachelor of Arts degree from Stanford in 1991, and received his master's degree in 1992.[6]

Cory Booker's education continued at the University of Oxford's Queen's College, where he—like 2020 primary opponent Mayor Pete Buttigieg—attended the Rhodes Scholar program, graduating in 1994. It was an important time in Booker's life because he made a longtime friend of Chabad Rabbi Schmuley Boteach, which led to his unusual role as president of the L'Chaim Student Society in Oxford, and furthered his lifetime learning about spirituality.[7] Boteach went on to become a famous author,

TV host, and public speaker, and the two men became close friends throughout during a more "innocent time." Sadly, that friendship was rent asunder by politics in 2015 when the senator supported President Obama's Iran nuclear weapons freeze agreement and Boteach called it an unforgivable betrayal of Israel, writing in the *Jerusalem Post* that "I will always love Cory as the man who became my closest friend. But I cannot overlook his stunning unfaithfulness to the Jewish people."[8]

Arriving home from Oxford, Cory Booker enrolled in the prestigious Yale Law School, where he started a L'Chaim Society chapter and graduated with a juris doctor degree in 1997. From there, he moved to a Newark and began practicing law for a housing nonprofit that organized tenants and fought for their rights. Two years later, he challenged the longtime incumbent city councilman in his district, the Central Ward; it had been the epicenter of Newark's violent riots in 1967, which left twenty-six people dead.[9]

Cory Booker took on former professional boxer George Branch, who was part of the existing political machine and a sixteen-year incumbent.[10] He calls the 2020 Democratic primary the most similar to that first, hotly contested race where nobody thought he had a chance to win. Branch finished 340 votes ahead of Booker in the general election. But Cory Booker used his fund-raising prowess and worn-shoe-leather approach to retail politics to grind out a ten-point win in the runoff. He won by turning out voters in the projects who had never voted before. Councilman Cory Booker was twenty-nine years old and brimming with ideas, but he faced a political machine and a generation gap at city hall that would only spur him on to more daring acts of political activism and launch his career in politics, ultimately leading him to the United States Senate in 2013 and to become a top contender for the 2020 Democratic nomination.

Senator Booker has never been married and has no children, but is currently dating actress Rosario Dawson, who is best known for her role in the hit movie *Men in Black*.[11]

CORY BOOKER GETS INTO A STREET FIGHT

Cory Booker gained a reputation as "almost too good to be true" from the time he became a Newark City Council member at age twenty-nine until he completed his first run for office in 2002, which was documented in the Oscar-nominated documentary *Street Fight* in 2005.

Longtime Newark mayor Sharpe James—who also served as the region's state senator, a form of dual office-holding only permitted in New Jersey—was seeking a fifth term in 2002.[1] Cory Booker's insurgent campaign united disparate elements of the city's population who were looking for change, and eventually led to his slate of candidates taking over city hall.

He didn't win that first race for mayor, but he presciently predicted on the eve of the 2002 election, that the effort would turn him into the front-runner for the 2006 race.[2] It did.

Early in his tenure, Booker rejected the status quo, but found himself outvoted 8-1 regularly. Amid great personal angst and a wave of violent crimes, he engaged in an act of protest that surprised his neighbors. He said it "changed everything."[3] Councilman Booker got fed up, pitched a tent, and went on a ten-day hunger strike to protest the administration. The *Washington Post* reported:

> "Within 24 hours, people were saying, 'You're not sleeping out there alone,' and eventually there were dozens of people sleeping under this huge wedding tent," Booker said. "The first morning of the strike, we had a prayer circle of four people. By the end, there were enough people for us to form a circle around the two buildings. Priests, rabbis, Latinos, blacks."
>
> The media showed up, Mayor James relented—just a little—and Booker started eating. "It really changed my perceptions about power," says Booker, who is wearing a blue oxford shirt and a yellow tie and speaking, as he always does, like a man in a rush. "It's not about the office that you hold or the money in your bank account. Real power never stems from agencies. It stems from spiritual power."

Booker also embraced some conservative ideas at the time, like school choice vouchers.[4] His campaign was mainly about his biography; opposing Mayor James made getting legislation passed virtually impossible.

Mayor Sharpe James was first elected as a Newark councilman in 1970, just three years after the landmark 1967 uprising, which happened while African Americans were on the way to becoming the majority in New Jersey's largest city by population. From 1940 through 2000, the city experienced a population shrinkage of 37,000 people, including over 70,000 nonwhite resident departures, according to census data.[5, 6]

Sharpe James won the mayorship that would define his political career in 1986, and he was a popular incumbent by the time Cory Booker took him on in 2002.[7] Along the way, Sharpe James added the title of state senator, which gave him a total government salary of nearly a quarter million dollars—at the time more than all fifty state governors—in a city with a 26 percent poverty rate.[8] The *Washington Post* called Mayor James's political machine as "formidable and oiled with jobs, rewards and retribution" as the political machine of white politicians he helped "smash" after taking office in 1970 and later defeating the city's first, four-term African American mayor.

Mayor James had the support of the state's Democratic establishment, and used his name recognition as well as his powers as the city's chief executive to do everything he could to keep that position. In turn, Booker used the network he built while attending Stanford, Oxford, and Yale Law School to amass an unheard-of $3 million war chest to fight the mayor.

Establishment opposition to Cory Booker's campaign grew out of the generation gap. Booker was the child of civil rights activists, but James—who is thirty-three years older—and his generation of politicians had lived through those battles. The *Post* reported:

> Booker calls himself the heir of the civil rights generation: They tore down barriers; now young blacks like him live the dream. "I stand on Sharpe James's shoulders," he says.

James, however, does not want him there. His machine is in overdrive. His ward headquarters are packed with volunteers nightly. Booker supporters report being suddenly cited by city code enforcers and denied business permits. City workers tore hundreds of Booker signs off public property, until a court stopped them. Both the state police and federal observers are being deployed to monitor today's voting. The Rev. Jesse L. Jackson, stumping with James, said Booker has a "sheeplike appearance and wolflike characteristics."

In return, Booker demands to know why, after 32 years under two black mayors, Newark does not have a vibrant cohort of minority contractors, lawyers and accountants. "The richest people in Newark are not businesspeople," he says. "They're politicians." African American celebrity scholar Cornel West and hip-hop star Queen Latifah are stumping with him this weekend, and Spike Lee is taping calls to voters, calling Booker "the right thing."[9]

Senator Booker finds himself fighting a similar generational battle in his own party for the 2020 Democratic primary, having watched the esteemed Rep. John Lewis support his opponent, Vice President Joe Biden, early in the race, when Booker spoke out against his close relations with revanchist southern Democratic senators in the 1970s.[10] For example, Jim McGreevey, then the governor of New Jersey, told a Martin Luther King Jr. celebration that reelecting Mayor Sharpe would guarantee a new arena for the New

Jersey Devils hockey team and the Nets basketball team, coming close to breaking a law prohibiting elected officials from promising official acts for votes.[11] (McGreevey later resigned in a scandal. The arena was built, but the Nets subsequently moved to Brooklyn).

Cory Booker landed a tremendous blow against his opponent when the powerful firefighters union local chose to endorse him over the incumbent to send a message to city hall.[12]

However, the example of Lewis choosing Biden is merely a battle of words; *Street Fight* got its name because the entrenched incumbent mayor literally pulled no punches to get his way, and not just with Cory Booker. Mayor James went to great lengths to kick out the documentary filmmaker numerous times, which any civil rights activist would recognize as a violation of the Constitution's First Amendment. In 2005, the Black Lives Matter movement was years away, but in retrospect, it's shocking to watch a Democratic politician deploying the weapons of censorship and police intimidation, especially against another Democrat. Officially, the race was nonpartisan.

Councilman Booker fought the election on the street, too, going door-to-door through some of Newark's most dangerous neighborhoods, the places where he had been living since graduating from Yale Law. James supporters focused on Booker's upbringing in Harrington Park, a suburb twenty minutes north of the city, looking at his parents' choice of homes (which was driven more by access when housing discrimination was freely practiced in America) to call the light-skinned younger man "less black" than his incumbent opponent.

Councilman Booker suffered the indignity of being kicked out of the city's subsidized housing projects by a government administrator who quickly attracted high-ranking police officials to hector him, even while complaining that the James campaign had been doing the same kind of door knocking and one-on-one voter discussions he was holding. Then, a trailer that served as one of the Booker campaign offices were broken into, and computers and strategic information were stolen. Nobody could prove who broke into the office.

All of that doesn't begin to explain the slanderous broadsides that Mayor James commonly tossed at Booker, falsely accusing him of being supported by America's worst white terrorist group in a campaign to "other-ize" the councilman.[13] The documentary is available to Netflix subscribers and goes into gory detail. Modern watchers might watch James and imagine a certain president who lies constantly and slanders his opponents as a form of bullying.

In turn, many of the personality traits—and quirks—that the public has come to know about Cory Booker were on full display during the campaign. The *New York Times Magazine* reported:

> A churchgoing Baptist, Booker also professes an interest in Buddhism and says that he meditates once or twice a day. He is a lifelong teetotaler, and he became a vegetarian in England after reading Gandhi. "He said, 'You have to be the change,'" Booker explained to me. "That's radical, to say you can live your life fully consistent with your beliefs."

Booker's intense interest in other cultures feels like more than glib politics; it is a theme that quickly emerges in conversation with anyone who has known him over the years. Booker's Jewish connection dates back to Oxford, where one night during his first year there he was invited by a friend to a dinner held by a Jewish group on campus called the L'Chaim Society. Booker remembers showing up, he says, "though I couldn't even pronounce the name. I entered this room full of Orthodox Jews and was like, 'O.K., I'm in the wrong place.' It was like that commercial where you walk into a room and the music stops and everyone turns to stare."

Booker's friend didn't show, but just as Booker was turning to leave, the wife of the rabbi who ran the group asked him to stay anyway and join them for dinner. Booker and the rabbi—a former Lubavitcher named Shmuley Boteach, who has gone on to become famous in his own right for publishing books like "Kosher Sex"— were soon deep in discussion. In the weeks that followed, they started trading books. "I would give him Baldwin and DuBois," Booker says, "and he would give me Hillel."

The next year, Booker, at Boteach's urging, became president of L'Chaim— its first (and only) non-Jewish, nonwhite student leader.[14]

Councilman Booker's intense ambitions were no different then, either. The *New York Times* reported that he was a bachelor who slept only five or six hours per night, pouring his energy into his work. Pundits were amazed at the intensity of the James-Booker race, which consumed the local airwaves in a manner reminiscent of statewide races.

Newark's largest daily newspaper, the *Star-Ledger*, endorsed Cory Booker "with enthusiasm" and attacked Sharpe James as out of touch with reality for touting the city as having experienced a renaissance, saying that, "Inefficiency reaches incompetence in City Hall."[15] The U.S. Attorney's Office for New Jersey—run by then-top prosecutor Chris Christie—sent monitors to oversee the election after the Booker campaign made a request for oversight in the face of James's dirty tactics.[16]

On election day, Cory Booker fell short by 3,500 votes, slightly less than a six-point margin.

"It was a no-holds-barred street fight that pitted a potent political machine—with its control of city jobs and a 16-year aura of invincibility—against a well-funded outsider running as reformer," wrote the *Star-Ledger*'s Ted Sherman. "The machine won."[17]

"We lost one skirmish tonight, but the battle continues," Booker told supporters at a local restaurant after the race was called for the incumbent, according to the *Star-Ledger*. "I was called many creative names during this campaign. But let me tell the entire city and *the nation* that I have only begun to fight for the people. I say: Batten down the hatches. Cory Booker is not going anywhere."[18] The crowd at Booker's election night party started chanting "We'll be back! We'll be back!" and he shut them down.

"We don't even need to say 'We'll be back,'" he told his supporters, "because we are not going anywhere."[19]

Street Fight by Marshall Curry was released at the Tribeca Film Festival on April 23, 2005, and on PBS television nationally three months later. The eighty-three-minute film lays bare the machine politics that dominated Newark in 2002. It won numerous film festival awards, as well as garnering nominations for both an Emmy and an Academy Award.

MAYOR OF NEWARK

ory Booker left public office in 2002 and went into private law practice, but he never stopped running for mayor. His prescient speech at the end of his first mayoral campaign turned out to be entirely correct. Booker went on to win the 2006 election to become the mayor of Newark at age thirty-seven after running a four-year-long campaign that raised over $6.6 million dollars and achieve an overpowering victory at the polls with 70 percent of the ballots.[1] The Booker campaign hired the same communications team that had represented the James in the last election, and raised funds for the other council races on his slate.

Incumbent mayor Sharpe James pulled out of the race eleven days after beginning his bid for a sixth term, while facing an FBI investigation into preferential land sales. The new mayor's "Booker team" slate of council candidates pulled off a clean sweep, earning seven of Newark's nine council seats.[2] Booker even defeated one of James's sons, who was trying to follow in the footsteps of his father. Just over two years later, U.S. Attorney Chris Christie convicted Sharpe James and his paramour on fraud charges, requesting a twenty-year sentence, but getting only twenty-seven months. He became the latest Newark mayor criminally convicted in an unbroken string going back to 1962.[3]

Mayor Booker took over a city with a surging crime problem, a large budget deficit, and a bloated workforce. When the first-term mayor looked to use professional discipline to remove recalcitrant employees, he discovered that the city entirely lacked any system of employee evaluations.

A year into the job, he candidly admitted to the *Star-Ledger,* "I'm worn. Everything is hard. I've been losing my temper more."[4] Booker won some victories on improving quality of life and installed an outsider police chief, but the city was struggling with double the regional unemployment rate during waning economic good times. In his first year, he had to raise property taxes to narrow the budget gap. "It's a grinding job, but I wouldn't want to be in any other place in my life," Booker told the Newark newspaper during an hour-long interview in his office at City Hall. "I get to be part of an incredible, gritty, tough, amazing city. And to be a mayor of a big city, you have to push on so many fronts. To gain on any inch of ground takes a lot of effort."[5] Homicides plunged from one hundred and seven in 2006 down to sixty-nine in 2008.

How bad was crime in Newark? A month into his term, Mayor Booker helped chase down a robber in front of city hall, whom he saw take a bag of money from a nearby bank customer.[6] Booker's security detail caught the fleeing suspect.

As the Great Recession landed in Newark, Booker faced tough decisions and had to lay off 163 police officers. Still, his national political profile continued to be expansive, and he did help change the perception of Newark in a significant way during his seven-year term of office and attracted a pair of major corporate headquarters, raised new investment into housing, and sparked the first significant population growth in decades. Both Audible.com and Panasonic moved into Newark, and Prudential Insurance began building a new tower there during his term as well.[7]

Mayor Booker's accomplishments included Teachers Village, the first residential development built from the ground up for professional educators. He lured Whole Foods to the city and cured some of its "food deserts," which are urban areas underserved by real grocery stores with fresh produce. Crucially, the Booker administration restored an element of professionalism to municipal decision-making for permits, which created a basis for growth that his successor used to the city's benefit.[8]

"A former Booker administrator said Booker implemented structural changes to Newark that were often hard to measure," NJ.com reports.[9] "'Solving all problems for all people is not a practical metric for urban and community development,' the administrator said. 'Some of that is longstanding and if people think that any one mayor is going to solve it, that is not realistic.'"

Newark's schools are supposed to be run by the city and its mayor, but were under the control of the state of New Jersey from 1998 to 2018. Cory Booker did attract a $100,000,000 investment into Newark's schools from Facebook founder Mark Zuckerberg in 2010, it wasn't a panacea, though a Harvard study found that it did help.[10] Booker's successor is a former high school principal and managed to regain local control of the system.

Cory Booker used his political platform as Newark's mayor to fight back against the city's image as a punching bag for late-night comedians—quite literally—when he "feuded" with Conan O'Brien, the former host of NBC's *Tonight Show*. The mayor had amassed a million followers on this Twitter account and realized that his audience was on par with the late-night TV show, so he decided to mobilize that audience to help the city.[11] Eventually, Hillary Clinton, then the secretary of state, stepped in to broker a peace between O'Brien and Booker.[12] After six months of friendly back-and-forth, Mayor Booker appeared on *The Tonight Show* in March 2010 to accept O'Brien's peace offering, a $100,000 donation to the charitable organization he promoted, Newark Now.[13]

Later that year, Mayor Booker made national headlines shoveling snow for one of his constituents after they reached out to him on Twitter and asked for help during the Great Blizzard of 2010.[14] To this day, Senator Booker still takes to the streets to lend a hand to random constituents during large snowstorms.[15]

Cory Booker raised over $7 million for his 2010 reelection campaign and earned 59 percent of the votes—an eleven-point drop from four years earlier—heading into his second term on the job.[16]

Still, by his fifth year in office, the *New York Times* reported that Booker's "sparkle has begun to dim." By October 2011, he had to testify against one of his closest allies, a former deputy mayor and bodyguard during the brutal 2002 "street fight" campaign. Even though the *Times* made it abundantly clear that the mayor's own honesty was "not in question," the proceedings took a toll on him.

By the end of Booker's term, homicides had increased from 68 murders up to 113 homicides in 2013; budget cuts to the police department cannot have helped there. Yet, as of mid-2019, Newark has turned around its notorious crime problem in the intervening years and recently hit fifty-year lows in a variety of categories of criminal offenses.[17]

As mayor, he raised property taxes to try and balance the city's budget, but in 2010 and 2011, the state had to provide emergency aid anyhow, something not uncommon for municipalities to do in the aftermath of the financial crisis a few years earlier. In Mayor Booker's last year in office, he left the city with a balanced budget for the first time, after calling out the city council very publicly in his State of the City address.[18] He went through multiple budget directors.

Cory Booker's detractors point out that much of the growth in Newark has happened in its downtown area, not its outlying districts. His record on fighting corruption was mixed, since he ended the city's old machine politics, but wasn't effective in overseeing his allies, whose problems exploded into a full-blown bribery scandal at the Newark Watershed soon after Booker left office, which we explore fully in chapters 8 and 9 as events unfolded chronologically.[19] "If not the most glaring black mark on his records," said a former *Star-Ledger* reporter about the mess "it's certainly one of them."

Mayor Booker struggled with his job approval inside the city at times, but outside the city he was revered; that is how he raised a quarter of a billion dollars in charitable funds and donations in just his first six years in office, much of it from donors twelve miles away in Manhattan.[20] That's why *Bloomberg News* concluded that, "the high-profile New Jersey mayor has already cultivated an enviable calling card: his ability to charm Wall Street." Pitching Newark as a "city of emergent hope," Booker attracted billions of dollars' worth of development in those years. *Governing* magazine wrote:

> In one sense, Booker did what all mayors try to do: fight crime, reduce poverty and expand economic development. Yet no other city of Newark's size could claim a mayor with Booker's national name recognition, a Twitter audience of 1.4 million followers, and friends that include Oprah Winfrey and Barack Obama. In short, Booker brought unusual resources to bear on his city's problems. Could the Supermayor rescue a national symbol of urban decline? It was a challenge Booker seemed to embrace wholeheartedly. "We started with a vision," he said in his state-of-the-city address in March, "that Newark would set a national standard for change—for transformation." This is the story of how Booker tried to set that change in motion.
>
> The city reported $1 billion in real estate development in 2011 and 2012—about a third of all development across the state in sheer square footage. Another $2 billion is in the pipeline for the next two years. Bolstered by a growing immigrant population, Newark finally bucked its 60-year depopulation trend in the 2010 Census. What Booker couldn't do with city resources, he sought to accomplish through public-private partnerships, attracting millions in philanthropic investments to further his policy agenda.[21]

It's fair to say that there are three different verdicts on mayor Cory Booker's time atop Newark's city government. Residents in the city's outer wards are not happy with Booker's job performance, because he did not deliver on the substantial promises he made to bring a transformational change to those neighborhoods, one of which he still lives in today. Booker entered government as a reformer, but saw many of his allies succumb to corruption, though his record as the only former Newark mayor to be clean himself speaks volumes about his character being upstanding. And it is totally undeniable that the city of Newark definitely benefited from Mayor Booker's tenure and leadership in the long run, because it marked an undeniable change for the better in the way that the "Brick City" is being run, which spurred significant economic and commercial opportunity.

BOOKER'S PATH TO THE SENATE

ory Booker's ascent from mayor of New Jersey's largest city to its junior senator was never assured, but the events of 2012 went a long way toward raising his national political profile. Due to events beyond his control, instead of the 2014 race he planned to run, Mayor Booker would campaign for and win his Senate seat in 2013.

In early 2013, Fox News personality Geraldo Rivera was publicly pondering a GOP run for New Jersey's Senate seat, and early polling from Quinnipiac University showed Booker winning 59 percent of the vote in a hypothetical matchup of the two. But Booker refused to formally declare for the race while the governor's contest was ongoing.[1]

On June 3, 2013, everything changed when Lautenberg's fifth term in the Senate ended prematurely when he succumbed to pneumonia at age eighty-nine.[2] The following day, Gov. Christie did something unexpected, callously political, and economically irresponsible: he declared a special election for the Senate seat would take place just nineteen days before the general election. The state spent twenty-four million dollars on the extra election because the Republican governor was afraid Booker would bring too many African American voters to the polls on the same ballot.[3]

Four days later, the mayor declared his Senate campaign from the new Newark headquarters of Audible.com—a company he attracted to the city—with an in-person endorsement from longtime former New Jersey Senator Bill Bradley. The *New York Times* reported:

> "We have changed a city, despite the cynicism of so many who believed that real change here in Newark was impossible," Mr. Booker said. "This is the truth of Newark, and I tell you right now that there is another city in America that needs some change. Too many have come to believe that Washington, D.C., is a place where nothing can get done, where people don't work together, don't compromise, don't make progress. People don't believe that Washington is a place that is sticking up for American families. This has to end."
>
> At the announcement, former Senator Bill Bradley, who like Mr. Booker is a Democrat who entered politics as an Ivy League–educated former Rhodes scholar, introduced the mayor-turned-candidate as "the right person for the right office at the right time," one who sees politics as "a noble enterprise, not a dirty business."

Cory Booker's opponents in the Democratic primary were a crème de la crème of the state's elected officials, including a pair of congressmen and the speaker of the state assembly. Yet, from minute number one until the votes were cast, Newark's mayor led in every significant poll with at least

49 percent of the surveyed voters' support. Sen. Lautenberg's widow endorsed one of his opponents, backhandedly insulting Booker in a press conference.[4]

But a week before the votes were cast, the *New York Times* revealed that Booker was the cofounder and largest shareholder of a private tech startup called Waywire, for which he raised $1.75 million of startup capital.[5] Among Waywire's investors were then-Google CEO Eric Schmidt and Oprah Winfrey, as well as LinkedIn cofounder Ried Hoffman. One of its board members—the fifteen-year-old son of CNN boss Jeff Zucker—resigned because of the campaign reporting. If Booker won the race, he'd likely have to divest himself of the shares. "The reality is this is a company other people are running," Booker said according to *Talking Points Memo*.[6] "I've been focused on being a mayor for the last year. As I said before, this is not a new story." He promised to place his shares into a "public trust."[7]

A few days later, the *New York Post* surprisingly revealed that Mayor Booker had received five checks from his former West Orange, New Jersey, law firm Trenk DiPasquale, one for each year between 2007 and 2011, while he was in public office.[8] The entire reason that the mayor quit the firm before taking office was to remove the appearance of impropriety. The *Post* revealed that the law firm earned $2 million in revenue from agencies overseen by Booker, and revealed its direct ties to the Newark Watershed, an opaque public-private company that managed the city's water supply and paid Trenk DiPasquale nearly $1.3 million. Booker told reporters that the payments were all disclosed and made to buy out his equity share as a partner in the firm for five years, pursuant to a confidential financial settlement; but the payments were not previously disclosed. And that wasn't the whole story.

That same day, a conservative news outlet unearthed an old column he wrote about the awkwardness of teenage dating for *The Stanford Daily* while in college in 1992.[9] Booker explained how those experiences opened his eyes to the existence of date rape—though that is certainly not what he described himself doing in his writing—penning a column of why he adopted a more progressive stance toward dating and consent while he was a college football player.

Still, none of that mattered to the Democratic primary voters who cast their ballots a week later. Of those eight major public polls, seven of them underestimated Booker's final vote tally of 59 percent of the primary votes on August 13, 2013. It was a decisive primary win, but he faced Steve Lonegan, a formidable establishment Republican candidate, in the general election.

It wasn't an easy general election race. Steve Lonegan worked hard to turn Booker's celebrity status, million Twitter followers, and late-night television appearances into a liability by highlighting the mayor's fund-raising trips to Silicon Valley.

Lonegan is the former mayor of the nearby village Bogota, only a fifteen-minute drive north from Newark. Amazingly, Lonegan had also attracted national attention for one of his mayoral campaigns—in part because he and another candidate in the race were both legally blind—and that election was featured in a documentary named *Anytown, U.S.A.*[10]

At the time, New Jersey's Republican party was experiencing a renaissance behind Gov. Christie in the longtime Democratic stronghold, though nobody yet knew that the former prosecutor had just sown the seeds of his political career's terrible end by closing the busy Fort Lee, New Jersey, bridge to Manhattan for political purposes.[11] Cory Booker's popularity in the state would be tested by a Republican opponent, who was at the time the state director of the conservative anti-tax group Americans for Progress.

A New Jersey state senator who was one of Lonegan's top backers decried the special election, but threw his support behind the former mayor, which apparently cleared the field.[12] Lonegan won over 80 percent of the Republican primary votes, although his primary had 65 percent fewer voters than the Democratic race.

Just under a month into the campaign, Booker stepped down from the company Waywire—which he founded—and donated his shares to charity.[13] Another New York tech company named Magnify Media purchased Waywire on the eve of the election, absorbing its technology, and rebranded itself to that name.[14]

Steve Rosenbaum, of Magnify Media, told the Associated Press in May 2019, "Booker's vision for Waywire was solid and remains relevant today. But he said Booker's role with the company was not sustainable once he started campaigning for the Senate, which happened earlier than he expected following Lautenberg's death. All of a sudden, it was pretty clear that he just didn't have the bandwidth nor was it the right thing for him to be running for U.S. Senate and also running a startup."[15]

Still, the existence of the company raised serious questions about the mayor's dedication to public service, though he pointed out that being an entrepreneur was a unique experience for someone in the public sector. It also raised questions about his closeness with some of the powerful interests whom he would have to oversee as the senator from New Jersey.

Mayor Booker's major claim to winning his office in 2002 rested on transparency, but the only reason that reporters discovered his side business was the greater level of disclosure requirements for Senate candidates. It's the same reason that the *New York Post* revealed that Booker earned $689,000 from his former law firm in a follow-up report right at the same time he was quitting his tech startup.[16] Instead of releasing his tax returns, the Booker campaign gave journalists three hours to review (and not to photograph) fifteen years' worth of the mayor's tax returns. Even still, *Post* reporters discovered some pretty sloppy paperwork, which indicated that Booker materially participated in the firm's business while in office, which would've required five hundred hours of work time that he obviously didn't do. While the revelations of Cory Booker's ties to his former law firm didn't derail his campaign or career in the Senate, they continued to linger as federal law enforcement agencies descended into the agency.

Luckily for the mayor, Lonegan ran a primarily negative campaign that didn't stick, focusing on his opposition to the Affordable Care Act, advocating a repeal of the Dodd-Frank Wall Street Reform and Consumer Protection Act, strong support of gun rights, and opposition to gay marriage.[17] The Republican candidate also published a shamelessly racially motivated immigration platform against "Illegal Alien Amnesty" while admitting that he himself was a second-generation son of immigrants. Lonegan's platform proved to be out of step with New Jersey's voting public.

Of the twenty major public polls conducted during the special election, nineteen showed Mayor Booker leading the special election over Lonegan, with all but one rating him as having 50 percent of the vote.

Only six days before the special election, Cory Booker suspended his Senate campaign when personal tragedy struck. His father, Cary Booker, died from the complications of a recent stroke he'd suffered at age seventy-six, after suffering from Parkinson's disease for many years.[18] Cary's life story featured prominently in Cory's political career. "A death ends a life, but not a love," tweeted the mayor the following morning.[19]

On October 16, 2013, Mayor Booker won the special election by nearly eleven points to become New Jersey's first African American US senator with 55 percent of the vote, outperforming the state's Democratic gubernatorial nominee by seventeen points when voters went to the polls just under three days later for the general election.

The forty-four year-old senator-elect would have to face the state's voters again just one year later to seek a full term of office.

THE JUNIOR SENATOR FROM NEW JERSEY

On October 31, 2013, Vice President Joe Biden swore Senator Cory Booker (D-NJ) into his new office with the state's senior senator Bob Menendez by his side.[1]

Senator Booker immediately began serving on three committees, two of which he still sits on today. His highest-profile assignment at the time was to the Senate Committee on Commerce, Science and Transportation, alongside posts on the Environment and Public Works panel and the Committee on Small Business and Entrepreneurship; the latter two positions he still holds through June 2019. In December 2016, the senator added a new, high-profile posting on the Senate Foreign Relations Committee, where he is the ranking member on a subpanel overseeing the State Department. He also sits on other subcommittees overseeing Africa, global health policy, and multilateral development issues.[2]

In January 2018, Senator Booker won assignment—at the same time his 2020 primary opponent Senator Kamala Harris (D-CA) was placed on the committee—to the powerful Senate Committee on the Judiciary after Democrats' shocking victory in an Alabama special election gave them one extra seat assignment.[3] The pair became the first African Americans serving on the Senate's judiciary panel in nineteen years, and that is when Booker left his assignment in the Commerce Committee. It's also the place where Senator Booker won his biggest bipartisan policy victory by pushing a major criminal justice reform bill past GOP's legislative "grim reaper," as Mitch McConnell fancies himself, in late 2018, when it became law.

BOOKER'S BIGGEST FIGHT: CRIMINAL JUSTICE REFORM

Senator Booker kept a relatively low profile in his first year in office—not unusual for a freshman senator in a body that prizes seniority above all else—but he began speaking out early in his first term to push for criminal justice reform, and has continued to make it one of his central policy positions in the 2020 Democratic primary. His biggest legislative victory in the field came at the end of 2018, when the First Step Act he originally cosponsored was passed into law with nearly universal acclaim.

It was no secret that Booker was in favor of reforming America's archaic marijuana prohibition laws. He said as much in a national news column and an AMA ("ask me anything") on Reddit in the run-up to his senatorial exploratory bid announcement, where he said he wanted to go beyond the current medical cannabis laws and called America's Drug War "big overgrown government at its worst."[4, 5] As he points out frequently, the United States has 25 percent of all prison inmates globally, but only 5 percent of the world's population.

The freshman senator became the primary cosponsor of the Record Expungement Designed to Enhance Employment Act of 2014 or REDEEM Act, his first major criminal justice reform bill in July 2014.[6] The sweeping bill would've created a new right to seek expungement or sealing of federal criminal records—including arrests without conviction and for a small number of criminal convictions—for nonviolent offenders who did not commit a sex crime where none exists, except for a minor provision of the Controlled Substances Act which criminalizes, drug possession. It would've also provided a mechanism to automatically expunge juvenile records when a crime wasn't committed and ban the use of solitary confinement for juvenile detainees except as a temporary response to impermissible behavior. Lastly, the bill would've ended the Clinton era's punitive ban on federal food and nutritional supplement benefits for people convicted of drug possession crimes.

While the REDEEM Act was read twice in the Senate and didn't pass, the senator from New Jersey didn't give up. The following month, he slammed the War on Drugs as a "tremendous failure driving poverty and [racial] disparity & not helping us achieve greater health or security," in a midsummer's Sunday-morning tweetstorm.[7] He had over a million followers as mayor, and his forceful condemnation of federal law enforcement crackdowns in medical marijuana states demonstrated leadership in the drive to end America's deleterious prohibition laws, which have only empowered drug cartels and wasted immeasurable tax dollars.

Today, every major Democratic candidate except for Vice President Joe Biden is firmly in favor of marijuana legalization. In 2013, it was considered an enormous political risk to take such a position, let alone during a reelection campaign in a state with a Republican governor who only months earlier said that New Jersey would never have legal weed, "so long as he was in office," even though the state had already had a medical marijuana law on the books for years by then.[8, 9]

These issues are sure to become a point of contention between Booker and his front-running 2020 primary opponent Biden, who passed many of the laws that led to mass incarceration during his time on the Senate judiciary committee and as its chair.

Senator Booker had to run for reelection in 2014, barely a year after winning his seat, and won with roughly the same vote share as his 2013 special election—though without significant Republican opposition—in a midterm election that was otherwise dominated by GOP victories elsewhere.

After his appointment to the Senate judiciary committee, Booker was instrumental in shepherding the First Step Act—which he cosponsored—through the partisan divide in Washington and into law at the end of 2018.[10, 11] "Our criminal justice system, as it stands right now, is an affront to who we say we are as a nation," Booker said on the Senate floor, according to the *Philadelphia Inquirer*. "We profess, we actually swear an oath to the flag, that we are a nation of liberty and justice for all, but our criminal justice system violates those values."

A coalition of groups advocating for the law say that it will help two hundred thousand inmates by allowing compassionate release, expanding time off for good behavior, and reducing some of the mandatory minimum sentences that resulted in mass incarceration.[12] First Step also requires that incarcerated women receive feminine hygiene products and limits the use of shackles on pregnant prisoners, as well as expanding reentry programs.[13]

And the act also extended the benefits of a 2010 justice reform to be retroactive and eliminated the infamous three-strikes law that fed mass incarceration both directly, and indirectly by spurring states to pass similar legislation.[14] Lastly, First Step finished what Senator Booker started in 2014, and banned the use of solitary confinement for juveniles under most circumstances.

"Our broken criminal justice system is a cancer on the soul of our nation that's disproportionately preyed upon low-income Americans, the addicted, and people of color," said Booker, explaining the urgent need to reform criminal justice in America.[15] "This bill is a meaningful step in the right direction that will help correct the ills of the failed War on Drugs."

The House passed the First Step act unanimously on a voice vote, and senators voted 87–12 in favor of the law, which President Trump signed into law on December 21, 2018, after being swayed by a national lobbying campaign.

HIS ROLE IN THE RISE OF THE RESISTANCE

As a senator, Senator Booker has never been afraid to respectfully challenge his colleagues. And it was his early leadership in the Resistance that helped spark the mass political movement that flipped forty seats in the House of Representatives in 2018, returning it to Democratic control. Two weeks after the 2016 election, Senator Booker posted this viral message to his Facebook page, where it provoked thirty thousand reactions:

We must always:
Be uncomfortable amidst injustice;

Disquiet in the face of wrongs; and
Disturbed as unfairness persists.

We must never allow bigotry to be easy; or hate to
  normalize
We must remain defiant
We must resist.

More dangerous than hate is apathy
More dangerous than bigotry is silence
And More dangerous than injustice is acquiescence to it.
Let us be resolved:
To be vigilant in the defense of others;
To be restless in pursuits of justice;
And let us never grow weary in the work of love[16]

Then, when Trump nominated former Alabama Senator Jeff Sessions to be the new attorney general, Senator Booker strongly disagreed with his choice, and spoke out forcefully. Senators tend to be extremely deferential to their colleagues, but he tweeted, "I won an election and am a U.S. Senator. Thus, I will use all my power to stop, fight and resist things that will hurt NJ and our nation."[17] Sessions had been previously denied an appointment to the federal bench in 1986 by a Republican-controlled Senate judiciary committee after a former employee blew the whistle on his open racism.

"Sen. Sessions's decades-long record is concerning in a number of ways, from his opposition to bipartisan criminal justice reform to his views on bipartisan drug policy reform, from his efforts earlier in his career to deny citizens voting rights to his criticism of the Voting Rights Act, from his failure to defend the civil rights of women, minorities, and LGBT Americans to his opposition to common sense, bipartisan immigration reform," he told *CQ Roll Call* on the eve of the contentious confirmation hearing, where he broke with tradition and testified against the Alabama senator in front of the Senate judiciary committee, something that had never been done before.[18]

"If one is to be attorney general, they must be willing to continue the hallowed tradition in our country of fighting for justice for all, for equal justice, for civil rights," said Senator Booker from the witness stand, highlighting a case where Sessions had used his power as a U.S. attorney to frivolously prosecute voting rights activists using the very law that is supposed to protect minority access to the polls.[19] "Sen. Sessions has not demonstrated a commitment to a central requisite of the job: to aggressively pursue the congressional mandate of civil rights, equal rights, and justice for all of our citizens. In fact, at numerous times in his career, he has demonstrated a hostility toward these convictions and has worked to frustrate attempts to advance these ideals. Persistent biases cannot be defeated unless we combat them. The arc of the universe does not just naturally curve toward justice—we must bend it."[20]

Four days after the president's tepidly attended inauguration, Cory Booker released a video urging Americans to resist the Republican Party's moves to issue executive orders that hurt middle-class people and to restart oil pipelines for the companies that lavished Trump and the Republican Party with oodles of campaign cash. The senator released a video on

Twitter captioned "The first days of the Trump Administration have proven that we must continue to resist" which exhorted Americans to stand up and fight in our darkest hours as a nation:

> I know there can be a temptation to feel overwhelmed. . . . We cannot let ourselves give in to even the temptation to despair or be cynical. We've got to keep going. We've got to keep fighting. I just want to encourage everybody to just remember that the power of the people is greater than the people in power. Don't surrender your power to feelings of overwhelm. Don't let this kind of stuff become normal so you feel numb to it.
>
> Get engaged. Every week. Try that. Every single week, commit yourself to taking some definitive action; to fight; to resist; to work against what is happening. If you do that and share it with others . . . it will inspire others, and lift us all.[21]

Little did Cory Booker know that just three short days later, he would have to take the lead in publicly fighting to roll back one of Trump's executive orders in what is to this day, one of the most dishonorable weekends in the country's history.

It all started on a Friday evening when President Trump issued an infamous executive order written by his white nationalist White House advisers that is colloquially known as the "Muslim ban," without informing anyone until it was issued. The newly sworn-in Republican president decided to ban people entry to the United States that hailed from seven countries whose religious majority is Muslim. The order was so poorly drafted that it even included people with green cards and proper permission to enter the United States, and thousands of travelers caught in mid-flight were detained at ports of entry, mainly at airports. It was a disaster. The ACLU and other civil rights organizations lept into action, filing five lawsuits.[22] Mass protests against President Trump's order targeting members of a religious minority group erupted at airports across the country, including at Newark Liberty International Airport, which is the sixth-largest international airport in the country.[23]

"We as Americans must stand up against Donald Trump's executive order," Senator Booker began in a Twitter video rallying the resistance to action, continuing:

> He is turning his back on our history, on who we are as a people. Our history is resplendent because that when people were in times of terror or facing persecution, when they were facing unbelievable horrors, we stood as a beacon of hope and light with arms open wide.
>
> Right in New Jersey we have Liberty's back on that statue, the "Mother of Exiles." We say give us your tired, your poor, your huddled masses, the wretched refuse of your teaming shores. The ideals of that statue are the ideals of our country."[24]

Senator Booker joined in a march at the Department of Homeland Security's Elizabeth (N.J.) Detention Center, near Newark Liberty International Airport, chanting, "No ban. No wall."[25] *USA Today* reports he told the crowd, "You don't ban immigrants, you let them in," Booker said to the crowd, urging them to continue protesting in peace. "This is a movement of love and not a movement of hate."

The following evening, Booker flew to Washington, DC, and gave a rousing address to the mass of gathered protesters at Dulles International Airport. He shared the results of one of the ACLU's lawsuits, which struck down Trump's executive order and let free the bewildered travelers who had permission to enter the U.S., but became unlawfully ensnared in the White House's pernicious dragnet.

> *This is not a one-night thing. This is not a one-day thing. I am telling you right now what were you're up against; what we've seen in the first eight days the Trump administration is that this is going to be a long, arduous, and tough fight.*
>
> *Let me right now let me tell you right now we have to be determined to continue the fight. I've been told now that the last of the people being detained will be released in the coming moments.*[26]

The assembled crowd at Dulles burst into loud applause at that moment, but the senator from New Jersey didn't stop there and joined forces with

the senior senator from his state to push back against the Trump administration's discriminatory border policies forcefully. Noting that three New
Jersey House Republicans broke with Trump on the executive order, they
promised to seek to defund the agencies engaging in extralegal detentions
at the border.[27] International arrivals at Newark—a major feeder airport
for Manhattan—dropped by 7 percent almost overnight in the wake of the
ban.[28] Ultimately, the issue was resolved in court after the Trump administration narrowed the order down significantly over three revisions to gain
court approval with a "waiver" program to allow reasonable exceptions,
instead of the all-out ban Trump first issued.[29]

A NEWARK SCANDAL THAT ENSNARED
BOOKER'S ALLIES FINALLY ENDS

Cory Booker's first campaign for Senate was accompanied by major reve-
lations about his personal finances due to the increased media scrutiny that
comes along with running for higher office. One of the top issues was his
role as the ex-officio chairman of the Newark Watershed, an agency dating to the nineteenth century that provided clean drinking water to five
hundred thousand residential subscribers and managed its sewers. Its
executive director Linda Watkins Brashear—a thirty-year veteran of the
agency—was caught in a massive bribery scandal. She was also a big ally of
the mayor's and a 2006 campaign volunteer.[30] One of Booker's former law
partners acted as a general counsel to the Watershed, on behalf of his former law firm. In September 2017, Watkins Brashear was sentenced to eight

years in federal prison for her role in the bribery scandal, and another project manager also got an eight-year sentence.[31]

Though Booker was nominally the chair of the agency by virtue of his mayorship, he never attended a meeting, and designated another official in his stead in 2010. Independent reporting on the agency criticized Mayor Booker for having time to attend paid outside speaking gigs, but not to attend the water agency's meetings. After an extensive investigation by a resident activist group and the *Star-Ledger*, the corporation managing the Watershed was turned over to a group of lawyers to find out what happened. They filed bankruptcy and, along with Booker's administration, dissolved the agency after its executive director's gambling problems and theft of funds from the agency were exposed; she had run the water utility like a giant slush fund.[32] Another ally of Booker, General Counsel Elnardo Webster II—the mayor's former business partner and campaign treasurer—had caused their old firm, and the firm he moved to later on, to pay over a million dollars in compensation for malpractice.[33]

The Newark Watershed agency Cory Booker inherited as mayor was so opaque that two and a half years after his Senate tenure began, lawyers were still arguing in court just to determine if it was a charity, a government entity, a private entity, or some hybrid of the three.[34] On June 16, 2016, Booker told *Politico* that he wasn't being vetted by the Hillary Clinton campaign as a potential vice presidential nominee.[35] Allegations related to the Watershed against Senator Booker were dismissed in June 2016.[36] Officially, the cloud over the senator from New Jersey was lifted. The following month, he stopped denying that the Clinton campaign was considering him for the ticket.[37] Still, the Watershed scandal turned what he called "one of his biggest policy losses" into a major ongoing blemish for the senator from New Jersey for the first few years of his tenure in Congress.[38]

LEGISLATIVE IDEOLOGY

An independent analysis of the bills that Senator Booker sponsored and cosponsored from 2015 through 2019 by the independent political website GovTrack.us rates him as the seventeenth most liberal member of the Senate.[39] In comparison, his opponents in the 2020 Democratic primary are Sen. Amy Klobuchar (D-MN), who is rated the thirty-fourth-most liberal senator, Sen. Elizabeth Warren (D-MA), who is ranked thirteenth-most liberal, and Sen. Harris, who is ranked fourth-most liberal. Sen. Bernie Sanders (D-VT) is ranked second-most liberal, while Sen. Kirsten Gillibrand (D-NY) is ranked the most liberal member of the Senate.

GovTrack's proprietary leadership rankings based upon how many bills he sponsored or cosponsored ranked him as submitting seventy-five bills in the 115th Congress from 2017 to 2019, which is the thirteenth most compared to all senators. Booker cosponsored over 517 bills—the seventh most of all senators—which indicates that he's willing to work collaboratively with others to achieve his goals. Their scorecard also reveals that six of his bills had a cosponsor in committee leadership who would oversee the bill. Two of those bills became law in the 115th Congress: the Action for Dental Health Act to expand access to oral hygiene to lower-income persons, and the 9/11 Memorial Act providing funding to organizations that commemorate the tragic terror attack in New York, Pennsylvania, and the Pentagon.[40, 41]

Senators Booker's bills had significant sponsorship in the House, with twenty of his bills sponsored in the lower chamber. Only six of his bills in the 115th Congress got voted out of committee.

Senator Booker missed twenty-eight votes out of the 599 votes in the 115th Congress, which is 4.7 percent of the total over the 115th Congress' two-year term. In contrast his opponent, Sen. Warren didn't miss any votes during that two-year period, Sen. Harris only missed two votes, Sen. Klobuchar missed three votes, and Senator Sanders missed fifteen votes during that same time period.

PREPARING HIS RUN FOR PRESIDENT

Senator Booker announced his presidential run in an email to supporters with a two-minute video on February 1, 2019, bypassing the "exploratory" phase of the race.

In the last twelve months, Senator Booker has filed these bills are relevant to his campaign:

- The Federal Jobs Guarantee Development Act to pilot a program that would lead to full employment for all who want to work.
- The Fair Chance Act, also known as the "Ban the Box" Act, which would help people with felony convictions reenter society by making it easier to get a job.

- The American Opportunity Accounts Act would fight income inequality by creating savings accounts for children known as "Baby Bonds."
- The Automatic Gunfire Prevention Act and the Assault Weapons Ban of 2017 are both acts proposing commonsense gun reforms.

He also cosponsored his opponent Senator Sanders's "Medicare for All" bill in February 2019, which would provide a "public option" as a means to strive toward universal health insurance coverage.

It's not unusual for a senator who is preparing a presidential campaign to attract significant attention for taking time away from their duties to prepare a national campaign. CNN reported that Senator Booker kept up a frenetic pace during the 2018 midterm elections, traveling to Wisconsin, Florida, Arizona, Alabama, Indiana, Montana, Georgia, Washington (state), Missouri, Minnesota, and Ohio.[42]

ANALYSIS: BOOKER'S CHANCES FOR WINNING THE NOMINATION AND PRESIDENCY

Cory Booker announced his 2020 Democratic primary bid on February 1, 2019, by releasing an emotional two-minute video to his supporters which he posted to YouTube entitled, "We will rise." He skipped the exploratory phase and chose that day because it is the kickoff of Black History Month, and the video spoke about finding a sense of common purpose in America. Booker would go on to officially launch his national campaign tour with a diverse crowd of 4,100 people at his rally on a sunny April afternoon in Military Park in his hometown of Newark.[1] Since then and leading up to the first Democratic debates, Booker remained in the small group of six front-running candidates polling consistently above 1 percent in Democratic primary field that has ballooned to twenty-five contestants as of June 2019.[2] Senator Booker raised $5 million in the first quarter of 2019, about a third of the amount his rivals hauled in, but with transfers from his Senate account maintained over $6 million cash on hand in the spring of 2019, suggesting a campaign that is disciplined about spending early.[3]

Booker is betting his campaign on his rhetorical mastery, his gleaming reputation as a "SuperMayor," and the retail political skills he mastered to rise through the ranks of New Jersey's rough-and-tumble politics. He stands to struggle from the Democratic primary's proportional representation system, which only gives delegates to candidates who win more than 15 percent of the vote, because his polling figures are consistently below the 10 percent mark in the early going, but if he breaks out of the field, it could serve to help his candidacy as the field winnows down.

"I want to start . . . by [thanking] my mother, it was her example all my life, her example of grace and courage and service; it's her love which the reason why I'm here today. I wish my dad could be here and in my heart I believe he is here," the former Newark mayor told his hometown supporters that April afternoon, while the chanted his name as he entered the stage.[4] "We're here today to seek justice. We're here today because we are impatient for that justice. And our sense of moral urgency, our impatience comes from the most demanding of all values. It comes from love. Love of our families. Love of our communities. Love of our country, and love of each other. You know, the mayor was right, Newark, 'Brick City,' this community . . . taught me all about that love." He continued:

> *It's not that feel-good easygoing love. It is strong coura-*
> *geous love. It is defiant love. The kind of love that works*
> *through heartbreak and pain and betrayal. It's the kind of*
> *love that keeps on going and never gives up. It's the kind*

of love that sacrifices, the kind of love that is essential to achieving justice.

I learned right here on these streets that you can't make progress by dividing people, you can't make progress by stoking fear, or setting us one against the other. I learned that the only way to overcome the really tough challenges is by extending grace, finding common ground, and working together. And we know this that today so many of us are hurting. So many of us are understandably angry. So many of us are feeling afraid for our futures and our families. Too many people believe the forces tearing us apart are stronger than the bonds that hold us together.

Well, I don't believe that; I believe we will bring our country together. I believe we will achieve things that other people say are impossible. I believe we will make justice real for all people, and that is why I am running for president of the United States of America.

And let me tell you . . . we are a great nation because of all our people into the people across the country who don't speak English as their first language I want to say to many of you many of you, "yo voy a hacer una Presidente para todo nuestra gente innuendo payees." I will be a president for all people in America.

When I arrived here in Newark over twenty years ago to work as a tenant rights lawyer, I found a city with challenges that some folks said were intractable. But we in Newark refused to believe that any problem is too hard to solve if we tackle it together. We were a community impatient for justice. Newark has always been a community impatient for justice, a community that knew, in the words of Dr. King, "wait has almost always meant never." And the communities like ours, and frankly in communities all across this country, wait still too frequently. Wait for clean water. Wait for decent paying jobs. Wait for better schools. Wait your turn.

Wait, well, here in Newark we refused to wait. When this incredible city took a chance on me as their mayor, the chief executive of this city, New Jersey's largest city, I didn't wait to start bringing people together. We didn't just talk about the injustice of families not having heat in the coldest months of the year; we took on the slumlords and doubled the rate of affordable housing production right here. We didn't just talk about the injustice, we didn't just wait to talk about the injustice of people not being able to buy fresh fruits and vegetables; we opened grocery stores in food deserts, we got people to invest here. We opened new businesses here. We created thousands of jobs here, together, and after sixty years of decline . . . look around you. Newark is growing again!

Cory Booker's ideology is one of a universal spiritual connection to people, pragmatic improvements in government, and an unabashedly progressive policy agenda married to his upbeat leadership in public office, despite the heavy challenges of governing. Senator Booker hasn't given a major campaign speech about foreign policy or released any documents yet, but as a member of the Senate Foreign Affairs Committee, he's known to be within the mainstream of Democratic political thought and is considered to be a pro-Israel lawmaker who doesn't subscribe to the Trump administration's more bellicose ideas.

His personal memoir, *United: Thoughts on Finding Common Ground and Advancing the Common Good,* is a *New York Times* best seller and takes readers inside the reason he's in public office and his plan to reoriented-orient American politics and our nation around compassion and solidarity.[5] Cory Booker is in favor of "Medicare for All," which his 2020 opponent Senator Bernie Sanders (D-VT) rereleased in early 2019. He cosponsored the Green New Deal proposed by Rep. Alexandria Ocasio-Cortez (D-NY), but has not put forward his own plan for dealing with manmade climate change yet.

At the end of June 2019, Booker is averaging seventh place in the seven major national polls, with a blended average support of 2.4 percent of respondents, according to *Real Clear Politics.* He has not led outright in any of the first fifty-four polls surveying the 2020 Democratic primary, with most polling showing his support at 2 to 3 percent in the saturated field of participants.[6]

A June 2019 poll in the key early primary state of South Carolina by the

Post and Courier shows 5 percent support for Senator Booker, good for sixth place.[7] The Palmetto state has the most African American voters of the four early states, and Booker must make a tremendous showing there to win the Democratic nomination. Since 1992, only former Senator John Edwards has won South Carolina's first-in-the-South primary and not gone on to hold the Democratic party's nomination.[8]

Booker is polling in the 2 to 3 percent range in New Hampshire[9, 10] In Iowa, the New Jersey senator has seen a polling spike as high as 6 percent, though most surveys show him in a similar range as New Hampshire.[11]

Booker didn't exceed the 1 percent mark—nor did most candidates— in an April 1, 2019, poll released by the Harvard Institute of Politics that surveyed voters aged eighteen to twenty-nine. That poll named Senator Bernie Sanders as the most chosen candidate by a landslide.[12]

Early Wisconsin polling in March 2019 showed Senator Booker in seventh place with 2 percent of the vote, but that primary contest is relatively late in the 2020 primary season and a lot has happened since that poll.[13] An early poll conducted in Florida by Bendixen & Amandi showed that Cory Booker was tied for fifth place with 1 percent of the vote, but 46 percent remain undecided in that survey, conducted one year out from the primary.

Booker will have to win South Carolina, and as well as winning a significant share of Iowa and New Hampshire's early primary delegates in order to make it into the final primary field before Super Tuesday, which kicks off the heavy schedule of primaries set for March 2020.

Senator Booker's list of endorsements by late May consists of one sitting U.S. senator—the senior senator from New Jersey—and all of the

Democratic U.S. Representatives from his home state, its governor, and, pointedly, his successor as mayor of Newark, who has been a fierce critic for years.[14] He also holds endorsements from multiple state legislators in Iowa and a roster of local officials as well as state legislators in South Carolina.

The first votes in the 2020 Democratic primary race will be cast in New Hampshire in the days leading up to February 11, 2020. Primary campaigns are dynamic by their nature, and most often the early front-runner does not capture the party's nomination.

Critically, *Real Clear Politics* average of the polling for a head-to-head matchup between Donald Trump and Booker shows the former vice president winning three out of the four tracked polls; Rasmussen, which typically favors the president, says Trump would win by 2 percent, which is within the polling margin of error.[15] A June 2019 Quinnipiac poll shows Booker beating Trump by five points, which is outside the margin of error. A Public Policy Polling survey taken in March 2019 showed Booker leading by seven points, and an earlier Emerson poll said Booker would beat Trump by two points, which is inside the margin of error. Head-to-head polls tend to correlate strongly with the concept of electability.

Booker has an objectively difficult path to becoming the Democratic nominee in 2020, but he has to convince the more liberal wing of the party that he'll fight for their policies despite his ties to Wall Street and donors from the pharmaceutical industry. If Booker only wins a plurality of pledged delegates, not a majority, going in to the Democratic National Convention, which would lead to a "brokered convention," then he could have a strong chance for superdelegates to give him the nod because of his record of loyalty to the party and generally good public relationship with

President Obama.[16] He's likely to be in the mix to be another candidate's running mate if he doesn't succeed in the primary, given his rhetorical expertise and hardworking style. However, it's hard to imagine the relentlessly positive and unity-driven Senator Booker in the traditional vice presidential nominee's role of "attack dog" who seeks to point out the negatives of the opponent's top of the ticket.

Cory Booker can definitely win the Democratic nomination, but he'll need to hone his message to primary voters and needs to pick a definitive ideological wing of the party to side with, either its moderate or its progressive base. His late June beef with Joe Biden elevated his campaign's profile sharply, and seems to signal that he's choosing the progressive track.[17]

Senator Booker has a tough road ahead of him, seeking to bring back the Democratic Party's "Obama coalition" of voters, when attitudes toward his top political benefactors are at their nadir in the party. This election's focus on electability makes Booker a potential choice to win the 2020 Democratic primary elections during a time when polls show 60 percent of Americans want a new president.[18]

NOTES

INTRODUCTION TO CORY BOOKER

1. Ross, Janell. "Six noteworthy things about Cory Booker." *Washington Post.* Last modified July 25, 2016. https://www.washingtonpost.com/news/the-fix /wp/2016/07/25/six-noteworthy-things-about-cory-booker/?noredirect=on &utm_term=.36a7ad329b15.

2. Jacobs, Andrew. "Evicted, Newark's Mayor Finds Another Blighted Street." *New York Times.* Last modified November 20, 2006. https://www.nytimes .com/2006/11/20/nyregion/20newark.htm.

3. Rebecca Buck. "Cory Booker Calls for Impeachment Proceedings to Begin." CNN. Last modified May 29, 2019. https://www.cnn.com/2019/05 /29/politics/2020-cory-booker-impeachment/index.html.

4. Parker, Kathleen. "Cory Booker's 'Spartacus' moment." *Washington Post.* Last modified September 7, 2018. https://www.washingtonpost.com /opinions/cory-bookers-spartacus-moment/2018/09/07/8c97eaee-b2f6-11e8 -aed9-001309990777_story.html.

5. Bump, Philip. "Cory Booker's Senate rules drama, explained." *Washington Post.* Last modified September 6, 2018. https://www.washingtonpost.com /politics/2018/09/06/cory-bookers-dramatic-violation-senate-rules-explained /?utm_term=.78a095095de7.

6. Boteach, Rabbi S. "Cory Booker: The Spiritual Senator." *Observer.* Last modified October 18, 13. https://observer.com/2013/10/cory-booker-the -spiritual-senator/.

7. June, Dave Q. "Cory Booker Hints at Wedding Bells with Rosario Dawson As She Joins Him for Talk Show Appearance." *People.* Last modified June 13, 2019. https://people.com/politics/cory-booker-hints-rosario-dawson -wedding-rupaul/.

8. Nagle, Molly. "Biden Says He Won't Apologize for Comments on Segregationist Democrats." ABC News. Last modified June 20, 2019. https://abcnews.go.com/Politics/vice-president-joe-bidens-comments-civility-working-segregationist/story?id=63809652.

9. Quilantan, Bianca. "Booker Maintains Biden Showed 'Lack of Understanding' in Segregationist Remarks." *Politico.* Last modified June 23, 2019. https://www.politico.com/story/2019/06/23/booker-biden-segregationist-remarks-1377063.

10. Hallerman, Tamar. "John Lewis Defends Biden Amid Segregationist Controversy." *Ajc.* Last modified June 21, 2019. https://www.ajc.com/news/state--regional-govt--politics/john-lewis-defends-biden-amid-segregationist-controversy/FgfjXNjO1rR8slj2cYBIjJ/.

11. Arke, Raymond. "Everything You Need to Know About Where Cory Booker Gets His Money." *OpenSecrets News.* Last modified February 13, 2019. https://www.opensecrets.org/news/2019/02/where-cory-booker-gets-his-2020-money/.

12. Samuels, Brett. "Booker to Stop Accepting Donations from Corporate PACs." *The Hill.* Last modified February 14, 2018. https://thehill.com/homenews/senate/373757-booker-to-stop-accepting-donations-from-corporate-pacs.

13. Nocera, Joe. "Zuckerberg's Expensive Lesson." *New York Times.* Last modified September 8, 2015. https://www.nytimes.com/2015/09/08/opinion/joe-nocera-zuckerbergs-expensive-lesson.html.

14. "Biden, Warren, Sanders Lead 2020 Field." Monmouth University Polling Institute. Last modified June 12, 2019. https://www.monmouth.edu/polling-institute/reports/monmouthpoll_nv_061219/.

15. Salant, Jonathan D. "Booker, Trailing in Polls, Says Early Front Runners Usually Don't Cross the Finish Line 1st." *Star-Ledger.* Last modified May 12, 2019. https://www.nj.com/politics/2019/05/booker-trailing-in-polls-says-early-front-runners-usually-dont-cross-the-finish-line-1st.html.

16. "Election 2020—2020 Democratic Presidential Nomination." *RealClearPolitics.* Accessed June 25, 2019. https://www.realclearpolitics.com/epolls/2020/president/us/2020_democratic_presidential_nomination-6730.html.

NEWARK'S "SUPERMAYOR" BECOMES A HOUSEHOLD NAME

1. "Newark Mayor Cory Booker Taken to Hospital after Rescuing Woman from House Fire." *Star-Ledger*. Last modified April 13, 2012. https://www.nj.com/news/2012/04/newark_mayor_cory_booker_taken.html.
2. "New Jersey Mayor in Fire Rescue." BBC News. Last modified April 13, 2012. https://www.bbc.com/news/world-us-canada-17700783.
3. Booker, Cory. Twitter. Accessed June 22, 2019. https://twitter.com/corybooker/status/190624173259890690.
4. Cory Booker. Twitter. Accessed June 22, 2019. https://twitter.com/search?q=%23CoryBookerStories&src=typd.
5. "Governor Christie and Mayor Booker: Don't Worry, We've Got This." YouTube. May 15, 2012. https://www.youtube.com/watch?v=wHN0ZeS5c-4.
6. Hohmann, James. "Booker Bristles at Bain Attacks." *Politico*. Last modified May 20, 2012. https://www.politico.com/blogs/politico-now/2012/05/booker-bristles-at-bain-attacks-124001.
7. Reeve, Elspeth. "Cory Booker's Private Equity Gaffe Is Going Great for Cory Booker." *The Atlantic*. Last modified May 21, 2012. https://www.theatlantic.com/politics/archive/2012/05/cory-bookers-private-equity-gaffe-going-great-cory-booker/327870/.
8. Kornacki, Steve. "Cory Booker, Surrogate from Hell." *Salon*. Last modified May 20, 2012. https://www.salon.com/2012/05/20/cory_booker_surrogate_from_hell/.
9. Tau, Bryon. "Booker Walks Back 'Nauseating' Comments." *Politico*. Last modified May 20, 2012. https://www.politico.com/blogs/politico44/2012/05/booker-walks-back-nauseating-comments-124038.
10. Haddon, Heather. "After Miscue, Refined Role For Booker." *Wall Street Journal*. Last modified August 14, 2012. https://www.wsj.com/articles/SB10000872396390444184704577587572165259022.
11. King, John, et al. "Democratic National Convention Officially Begins." CNN. Accessed via Nexis.com on June 21, 2019.
12. "Effects of Hurricane Sandy in New Jersey." Wikipedia. Last modified October 30, 2012. https://en.wikipedia.org/wiki/Effects_of_Hurricane_Sandy_in_New_Jersey.
13. Levy, Gabrielle. "Super Mayor Cory Booker Takes on Superstorm Sandy, One Crisis at a Time." UPI. Last modified October 30, 2012. https://www.upi.com/blog/2012/10/30/Super-mayor-Cory-Booker-takes-on-Superstorm-Sandy-one-crisis-at-a-time/5291351611808/.

14. Locker, Melissa. "Cory Booker Finally Solves Newark's Hot Pockets Crisis." *Time*. Last modified November 8, 2012. http://newsfeed.time.com/2012/11/08/newark-mayor-cory-booker-delivers-hot-pockets/.

15. Kasperowicz, Pete. "Chris Christie Explains How He Got Obama's Direct Phone Number." *Washington Examiner*. Last modified August 30, 2017. https://www.washingtonexaminer.com/chris-christie-explains-how-he-got-obamas-direct-phone-number.

16. "Chris Christie Can't Stop Praising Obama for Hurricane Sandy Efforts." YouTube. October 30, 2012. Accessed June 22, 2019. https://www.youtube.com/watch?v=EqwO9mtt14k.

17. Zernike, Kate. "In Stunning About-face, Chris Christie Heaps Praise on Obama." *New York Times*. Last modified October 31, 2012. https://www.nytimes.com/2012/11/01/nyregion/in-stunning-about-face-chris-christie-heaps-praise-on-obama.html.

18. Kasperowicz, Pete. "Chris Christie Explains How He Got Obama's Direct Phone Number." *Washington Examiner*. Last modified August 30, 2017. https://www.washingtonexaminer.com/chris-christie-explains-how-he-got-obamas-direct-phone-number.

19. Daunt, Tina. "Obama Brokers Peace Between Chris Christie and Bruce Springsteen." *The Hollywood Reporter*. Last modified November 5, 2012. https://www.hollywoodreporter.com/news/obama-springsteen-chris-christie-president-386626.

20. Glueck, Katie. "Booker OK with Gov's Obama Love." *Politico*. Last modified October 31, 2012. https://www.politico.com/story/2012/10/booker-ok-with-govs-obama-love-083090.

21. "A Year after Hurricane Sandy: New Jersey Recovery by the Numbers." FEMA.gov. Last modified October 25, 2013. https://www.fema.gov/news-release/2013/10/25/year-after-hurricane-sandy-new-jersey-recovery-numbers.

22. Auciello, Justin. "N.J. Announces Update on Recovery Programs for Displaced Sandy Victims." *WHYY*. April 8, 2019. https://whyy.org/articles/n-j-expands-recovery-programs-for-displaced-sandy-victims/.

23. Memmot, Mark. "Living On Food Stamps: Newark Mayor Cory Booker Takes Up Challenge." NPR. December 4, 2012. https://www.npr.org/sections/thetwo-way/2012/12/04/166475063/living-on-food-stamps-newark-mayor-cory-booker-starts-challenge-today.

24. Miller, Sarah. "How Did Newark Mayor Cory Booker Do on His Food Stamp Challenge?" Grist. Last modified December 11, 2012. https://grist .org/food/how-did-newark-mayor-cory-booker-do-on-his-food-stamp -challenge/.

25. "Cory Booker: I'll Explore U.S. Senate Run." *Star-Ledger*. Last modified December 21, 2012. http://blog.nj.com/njv_guest_blog/2012/12/cory _booker_senate_run_op-ed.html.

26. Cramer, Ruby. "Frank Lautenberg Retires To Avoid The 'Silly Season.'" BuzzFeed News. Last modified February 14, 2013. https://www.buzzfeednews .com/article/rubycramer/frank-lautenberg-retirement.

27. To continue reading this book chronologically, see chapter 8.

CAMPAIGN PLATFORM

1. "Sanders, 14 Senators Introduce Medicare for All." Sen. Bernie Sanders. Last modified April 10, 2019. https://www.sanders.senate.gov/newsroom /press-releases/sanders-14-senators-introduce-medicare-for-all.

2. Booker, Cory. "I Support Medicare for All Because Health Care is a Civil Right, a Human Right." *Medium*. Last modified September 11, 2017. https://medium.com/@SenBooker/i-support-medicare-for-all-because-health -care-is-a-civil-right-a-human-right-31675eb30be5.

3. Booker, Cory. Twitter. Accessed June 24, 2019. https://twitter.com /CoryBooker/status/1105287625521459201.

4. Sullivan, Peter. "Booker Tries to Shake Doubts About Pharmaceutical Ties Ahead of 2020." *The Hill*. Last modified January 14, 2019. https://thehill .com/homenews/campaign/424993-booker-tries-to-shake-doubts-about -pharmaceutical-ties-ahead-of-2020.

5. Booker, Cory. "Booker Joins Sanders, Blumenthal, and Colleagues to Introduce Sweeping Plan to Lower Drug Prices." Cory Booker Senate web-site. Last modified January 10, 2019. https://www.booker.senate.gov/?p =press_release&id=882.

6. Booker, Cory. "New Booker Bill Seeks to Establish Model for Federal Jobs Guarantee Program in High-Unemployment Communities." Cory Booker Senate website. Last modified April 20, 2018. https://www.booker.senate .gov/?p=press_release&id=778.

7. Booker, Cory. "Booker's Bipartisan 'Ban the Box' Bill Sails through House Committee." Cory Booker Senate website. Last modified March 26, 2019. https://www.booker.senate.gov/?p=press_release&id=907.

8. Booker, Cory. "Booker, Johnson, Cummings, Collins Introduce Bipartisan Legislation to 'Ban the Box.'" Cory Booker Senate website. Last modified February 7, 2019. https://www.booker.senate.gov/?p=press_release&id=888.

9. Booker, Cory. "Booker Announces New Bill Aimed at Combating Wealth Inequality." Cory Booker Senate website. Last modified October 22, 2018. https://www.booker.senate.gov/?p=press_release&id=861.

10. Yi, Karen. "Booker: It's Un-American for Full-time Workers to Live in Poverty." *Star-Ledger*. Last modified May 20, 2017. https://www.nj.com /essex/2017/05/sen_booker_rallies_for_newark_airport_workers_wage .html.

11. McCammond, Alexi. "Cory Booker Proposes Dramatic Expansion to Earned Income Tax Credit." *Axios*. Last modified April 15, 2019. https:// www.axios.com/cory-booker-2020-election-tax-policy-economic-plan -f51388bc-93ab-4b0b-a590-2404f44283c6.html.

12. Booker, Cory. "Booker, Clyburn Introduce Bicameral Legislation to Fight Poverty in America." Cory Booker Senate website. Last modified October 3, 2018. https://www.booker.senate.gov/?p=press_release&id=856.

13. Booker, Cory. "Booker, Menendez Join Senators in Introducing Common Sense Gun Laws." Cory Booker Senate website. Last modified October 10, 2017. https://www.booker.senate.gov/?p=press_release&id=674.

14. Booker, Cory. "Booker Joins Dem Senators in Introducing Assault Weapons Ban." Cory Booker Senate website. Last modified November 8, 2017. https://www.booker.senate.gov/?p=press_release&id=696.

15. Menendez, Bob. "Menendez, Booker, Colleagues Introduce Background Check Expansion Act to Reduce Gun Violence." Bob Menendez Senate website. Last modified January 7, 2019. https://www.menendez.senate.gov /news-and-events/press/menendez-booker-colleagues-introduce-background -check-expansion-act-to-reduce-gun-violence-.

16. Booker, Cory. "Cory's Plan to End the Gun Violence Epidemic." *Medium*. Last modified May 6, 2019. https://medium.com/@corybooker/corys-plan -to-end-the-gun-violence-epidemic-ab377d9fb112.

17. "Cory Booker's Dangerous Gun-Control Plan." *NRA-ILA*. Accessed June 24, 2019. https://www.nraila.org/articles/20190509/cory-booker-s-dangerous -gun-control-plan.

18. "Fact Check: Have Firearm Homicides and Suicides Dropped Since Port Arthur as a Result of John Howard's Reforms?" ABC News. Last modified April 29, 2016. https://www.abc.net.au/news/2016-04-28/fact-check-gun -homicides-and-suicides-john-howard-port-arthur/7254880.

19. Booker, Cory. "Cory's Firearm Suicide Prevention Plan." *Medium.* Last modified May 14, 2019. https://medium.com/@corybooker/corys-firearm -suicide-prevention-plan-9fa1f47d48c6.

20. Booker, Cory. "The Next Step Act." *Medium.* Last modified March 8, 2019. https://medium.com/@corybooker/the-next-step-act-34c29b4532bc.

21. Booker, Cory. "Restoring Justice." *Medium.* Last modified June 20, 2019. https://medium.com/@corybooker/restoring-justice-27eb6f6fbc90.

22. Booker, Cory. "Booker, Harris Statement on Senate Passage of Anti-Lynching Bill." Cory Booker Senate website. Last modified December 19, 2018. https://www.booker.senate.gov/?p=press_release&id=876.

23. Chappell, Carmin. "Cory Booker Introduces Bill to Legalize Marijuana Nationwide, with Support from Fellow 2020 Candidates." CNBC. Last modified February 28, 2019. https://www.cnbc.com/2019/02/28/cory-booker -introduces-bill-to-legalize-marijuana-nationwide.html?__source=twitter %7Cmain.

24. Booker, Cory. "Booker Announces Introduction of Bill to Form Commission for Study of Reparation Proposals for African-Americans." Cory Booker Senate website. Last modified April 8, 2019. https://www .booker.senate.gov/?p=press_release&id=901.

25. Booker, Cory. "Booker Reparations Bill Reaches 12 Senate Cosponsors." Cory Booker Senate website. Last modified June 14, 2019. https://www .booker.senate.gov/?p=press_release&id=937.

26. Booker, Cory. "How I Will Take Immediate Action to Protect Reproductive Rights As President." *Medium.* Last modified May 22, 2019. https://medium .com/@corybooker/how-i-will-take-immediate-action-to-protect-reproductive -rights-as-president-fd7f5d28f616.

27. Seung Min Kim. "Warren and Booker Polish Their 2020 Resumes." *Politico.* Last modified December 15, 2016. https://www.politico.com/story /2016/12/elizabeth-warren-cory-booker-committee-assignments-232691.

28. "Nuclear Weapon Free Iran Act of 2013 (2013 - S. 1881)." GovTrack.us. Accessed June 24, 2019. https://www.govtrack.us/congress/bills/113/s1881.

29. Booker, Cory. "Cory's Plan to Provide Safe, Affordable Housing for All Americans." *Medium.* Last modified June 5, 2019. https://medium.com

/@corybooker/corys-plan-to-provide-safe-affordable-housing-forall
-americans-da1d83662baa.

30. Lind, Dara. "Exclusive: Booker, House Dems Introduce Most Ambitious
Bill Yet to Curb Immigration Detention." *Vox*. Last modified April 30,
2019. http://vox.com/2019/4/30/18523745/cory-booker-immigration
-democrats-dignity-detained-act.

31. Booker, Cory. "Cory Reintroduces His Plan to Curb Immigration
Detention." *Medium*. Last modified May 1, 2019. https://medium.com
/@corybooker/cory-reintroduces-his-plan-curb-immigration-detention
-2b6720d8112b.

32. Booker, Cory. Twitter. Accessed June 24, 2019. https://twitter.com
/CoryBooker/status/1123346316787093505?ref_src=twsrc%5Etfw
%7Ctwcamp%5Etweetembed%7Ctwterm%5E1123346316787093505
&ref_url=https%3A%2F%2Fmedium.com%2Fmedia
%2Fd56bcf7ddd3a984ccc04d78f1a0ef69f%3FpostId%3D2b6720d8112b.

33. Bernal, Rafael. "Senate Dems Introduce Bill to Keep DACA Info Private."
The Hill. Last modified January 22, 2019. https://thehill.com/homenews
/senate/426478-senate-dems-introduces-bill-to-keep-daca-info-private.

34. Booker, Cory. "Booker, Norcross, Pascrell Announce Major Legislation to
Address Teacher Shortage." Cory Booker Senate website. Last modified
February 6, 2018. https://www.booker.senate.gov/?p=press_release&id=743.

35. Douglas-Gabriel, Danielle. "Education Department Rejects Nearly All
Applicants for a Student Loan Forgiveness Program." *LA Times*. Last modified April 3, 2019. https://www.latimes.com/business/la-fi-student-loan
-forgiveness-education-department-betsy-devos-20190403-story.html.

36. "HSLF: Humane Scorecard." Humane Society Legislative Fund. Accessed
June 24, 2019. http://www.hslf.org/our-work/humane-scorecard.html.

BIOGRAPHY: FORMATIVE BACKGROUND AND EDUCATION

1. Booker, Cory. "Cory's Plan to Provide Safe, Affordable Housing for All
Americans." *Medium*. Last modified June 5, 2019. https://medium.com
/@corybooker/corys-plan-to-provide-safe-affordable-housing-forall
-americans-da1d83662baa.

2. Gilgoff, Dan. "Newark Mayor Cory Booker's Course on World Religions."
U.S. News & World Report. Last modified August 7, 2009. https://

www.usnews.com/news/blogs/god-and-country/2009/08/07/newark
-mayor-cory-bookers-course-on-world-religions-in-hebrew-and-english.

3. Ibid.

4. Moriarty, Morgan. "Cory Booker: an Elite CFB Recruit Who Didn't Quite
    Pan out." *SBNation.com.* Last modified February 1, 2019. https://www
    .sbnation.com/college-football-recruiting/2019/2/1/18207178/cory-booker
    -football-career.

5. Moreno, Eric. "Senator Cory Booker Attributes His Success to Football."
    USA Football Blogs. Accessed June 25, 2019. https://blogs.usafootball.com
    /blog/6836/senator-cory-booker-attributes-his-success-to-football.

6. "BOOKER, Cory Anthony Biographical Information." United States
    Congress. Accessed June 25, 2019. http://bioguide.congress.gov/scripts
    /biodisplay.pl?index=B001288.

7. Boteach, Rabbi S. "Cory Booker: The Spiritual Senator." *Observer.* Last
    modified October 18, 13. https://observer.com/2013/10/cory-booker-the
    -spiritual-senator/.

8. Sullivan, Kevin. "Cory Booker and the orthodox rabbi were like brothers.
    Now they don't speak." *Washington Post.* Last modified May 21, 2019.
    https://www.washingtonpost.com/politics/2019/05/31/cory-booker-orthodox
    -rabbi-were-like-brothers-now-they-dont-speak/?utm_term=.9a6dfccb013a.

9. "1967 Newark Riots." Wikipedia. Last modified April 4, 2005. https://
    en.wikipedia.org/wiki/1967_Newark_riots.

10. Path, Simone. "Has Booker's Jersey Political Experience Prepared Him to
    Take on Trump?" *Chicago Tribune.* Last modified June 19, 2019. https://
    www.chicagotribune.com/sns-tns-bc-booker-nj-20190619-story.html.

11. "Rosario Dawson Confirms She's Dating Cory Booker, Says They're in
    Love." *TMZ.* Last modified March 14, 2019. https://www.tmz.com/2019
    /03/14/rosario-dawson-cory-booker-confirm-dating-amazing-president/.

CORY BOOKER GETS INTO A STREET FIGHT

1. "Dual Office Holding: Restrictions on Legislators." National Conference of
    State Legislatures. Last modified January 29, 2018. http://www.ncsl.org
    /research/ethics/restrictions-on-holding-concurrent-office.aspx.

2. Russakoff, Dale. "In Newark Race, Black Political Visions Collide."
    Washington Post. Last modified May 14, 2002. https://www.washingtonpost

.com/archive/politics/2002/05/14/in-newark-race-black-political-visions
-collide/9b4f2176-f560-420d-859c-76beebe23700/?utm_term=
.2c7f309b97d3.

3. Segal, David. "How Cory Booker Became Newark's Mayor: By Being Almost Too Good to Be True." *Washington Post.* Last modified June 3, 2006. www.washingtonpost.com/wp-dyn/content/article/2006/07/02/AR2006070200814_pf.html.

4. Tepperman, Jonathan D. "Complicating the Race." *New York Times.* Last modified April 28, 2002. https://www.nytimes.com/2002/04/28/magazine/complicating-the-race.html.

5. "New Jersey - Race and Hispanic Origin for Selected Large Cities and Other Places: Earliest Census to 1990." Census.gov. Accessed June 25, 2019. https://www.census.gov/population/www/documentation/twps0076/NJtab.pdf.

6. "Newark, New Jersey." Wikipedia. Last modified August 3, 2002. https://en.wikipedia.org/wiki/Newark,_New_Jersey.

7. "Sharpe James." Wikipedia. Last modified October 10, 2004. https://en.wikipedia.org/wiki/Sharpe_James.

8. Russakoff, Dale. "In Newark Race, Black Political Visions Collide." *Washington Post.* Last modified May 14, 2002. https://www.washingtonpost.com/archive/politics/2002/05/14/in-newark-race-black-political-visions-collide/9b4f2176-f560-420d-859c-76beebe23700/?utm_term=.c9ba388fdff1.

9. Russakoff, Dale. "In Newark Race, Black Political Visions Collide." *Washington Post.* Last modified May 14, 2002. https://www.washingtonpost.com/archive/politics/2002/05/14/in-newark-race-black-political-visions-collide/9b4f2176-f560-420d-859c-76beebe23700/?utm_term=.c9ba388fdff1.

10. Litvan, Laura. "Civil-Rights Icon John Lewis Defends Biden's Segregationist Comments." *Bloomberg.* Last modified June 21, 2019. https://www.bloomberg.com/news/articles/2019-06-21/civil-rights-icon-lewis-defends-biden-s-segregationist-comments.

11. Stewart, Nikita. "GOP says McGreevey comments went too far: Governor assailed for linking James' reelection to new arena." *Star-Ledger.* January 23, 2002. Accessed June 24, 2019, via Nexis.com.

12. Stewart, Nikita and Mays, Jeffrey C. "Firefighters union stands alone with Booker." *Star-Ledger.* April 19, 2002. Accessed June 24, 2019, via Nexis.com.

13. Tepperman, Jonathan D. "Complicating the Race." *New York Times.* Last modified April 28, 2002. https://www.nytimes.com/2002/04/28/magazine /complicating-the-race.html.

14. Ibid.

15. Editorial Board. "Cory Booker for Mayor." *Star-Ledger.* May 2, 2002. Accessed June 24, 2019, via Nexis.com.

16. Martin, John P., Brown, Kimberly and Jordan, George E. "Federal monitors will watch over Newark election." *Star-Ledger.* May 11, 2002. Accessed June 24, 2019 via Nexis.com.

17. Sherman, Ted. "James proves it's good to be incumbent." *Star-Ledger.* May 15, 2002. Accessed June 24, 2019, via Nexis.com.

18. Brown, Kimberly, Mays, Jeffery C. And, Mueller, Mark. "It's still Mayor James." *Star-Ledger.* May 15, 2002. Accessed June 24, 2019, via Nexis.com.

19. Gibson, David, Mays, Jeffery C. And, Mueller, Mark. "Booker's loss does little to dim his potential." *Star-Ledger.* May 15, 2002. Accessed June 24, 2019, via Nexis.com.

MAYOR OF NEWARK

1. Sherman, Ted. "Before day of triumph, years of canny spending." *Star-Ledger.* May 10, 2006. Accessed June 24, 2019 via Nexis.com.

2. Mays, Jeffery C. And, Wang, Katie. "Booker's loss does little to dim his potential." *Star-Ledger.* June 15, 2006. Accessed June 24, 2019, via Nexis.com.

3. Baldwin, Tom. "Ex-Newark mayor gets 27 months for corruption." Asbury Park Press. July 29, 2008. Accessed June 24, 2019, via Nexis.com.

4. Mays, Jeffery C. And, Wang, Katie. "Booker's first year a wearying jour-ney." *Star-Ledger.* July 1, 2007. Accessed June 24, 2019, via Nexis.com.

5. Ibid.

6. "Newark Mayor Helps Nab Suspect Who Robbed Customer at Broad Street Bank." News 12 New Jersey. Last modified July 14, 2006. http://newjersey .news12.com/story/34880581/newark-mayor-helps-nab-suspect-who-robbed -customer-at-broad-street-bank.

7. J. B. Wogan. "But What Did Cory Booker Actually Accomplish in Newark?" *Governing.* Last modified December 1, 2013. https://www.governing.com /topics/politics/gov-what-cory-booker-accomplished.html.

8. Yi, Karen. "Now Everybody is Talking About Cory Booker's Time as Mayor of Newark. But How Did He Do?" *Star-Ledger.* Last modified February 5, 2019. https://www.nj.com/essex/2019/02/now-everybody-is -talking-about-cory-bookers-time-as-mayor-of-newark-but-how-did-he -do.html.

9. Ibid.

10. Yi, Karen. "Did Newark's School Reform Efforts Work? This Study Takes a Look." *Star-Ledger.* Last modified October 16, 2017. https://www.nj.com /essex/index.ssf/2017/10/did_newarks_school_reform_efforts_work_this _study.html.

11. ADAge. "How Cory Booker Saved Newark From Conan O'Brien Using Social Media." *Advertising & Marketing Industry News.* Last modified May 1, 2013. https://adage.com/article/special-report-digital-conference/cory -booker-saved-newark-conan-o-brien/241200.

12. Leo, Alex. "Hillary Clinton Intervenes In Conan O'Brien-Cory Booker Feud (VIDEO)." *HuffPost.* https://www.huffpost.com/entry/hillary-clinton -intervene_n_315059.

13. Epstein, Victor. "Facetious Feuding: Cory Booker & Conan O'Brien Quash the Beef On the 'Tonight Show.'" *HuffPost.* n.d. https://www.huffpost.com /entry/cory-booker-conan-obrien_n_324619.

14. Gregory, Sean. "Breaking News, Analysis, Politics, Blogs, News Photos, Video, Tech Reviews." *Time.* Last modified December 29, 2010. http:// content.time.com/time/nation/article/0,8599,2039945,00.html.

15. Adomaitis, Greg. "Cory Booker's Shoveling Again—This Time in Camden." *Star-Ledger.* Last modified January 26, 2016. https://www.nj .com/camden/2016/01/sen_bookers_camden_county_visit_includes_flood _dam.html.

16. "Cory Booker is Re-elected as Newark Mayor for Second Term." *Star-Ledger.* Last modified May 12, 2010. https://www.nj.com/news/2010/05 /cory_booker_reelected_as_newar.html.

17. Moriarty, Thomas. "Newark Sees Greatest Crime Drop in Nearly 50 Years, Officials Say." *Star-Ledger.* Last modified December 27, 2016. https://www .nj.com/essex/2016/12/newark_crime_down_in_2016.html.

18. Whitlow, Joan. "Booker, Newark City Council Acting As Foes, Not Teammates." *New Jersey Star-Ledger.* Last modified March 9, 2012. http:// blog.nj.com/njv_joan_whitlow/2012/03/booker_newark_city_council_act .html.

19. See chapters 8 and 9.
20. Bloomberg News. "Cory Booker's Charm Makes Friends for Newark on Wall Street." *Star-Ledger*. Last modified October 3, 2012. https://www .nj.com/business/2012/10/cory_bookers_charm_has_him_mak.html.
21. Governing. "But What Did Cory Booker Actually Accomplish in Newark?" *Governing*. Last modified December 1, 2013. https://www.governing.com /topics/politics/gov-what-cory-booker-accomplished.html.

BOOKER'S PATH TO THE SENATE

1. Cramer, Ruby. "Cory Booker Still Won't Confirm His Run For Senate." BuzzFeed News. Last modified February 22, 2013. https://www .buzzfeednews.com/article/rubycramer/cory-booker-im-not-bonding-myself -to-senate-run.
2. Brown, Emma. "Sen. Frank Lautenberg, five-term New Jersey Democrat, dies at 89." *Washington Post*. Last modified June 3, 2013. https://www .washingtonpost.com/local/obituaries/sen-frank-lautenberg-five-term-new -jersey-democrat-dies-at-89/2013/06/03/c8b60c8e-c5da-11df-94e1 -c5afa35a9e59_story.html.
3. "2013 United States Senate Special Election in New Jersey." Wikipedia. Last modified June 3, 2013. https://en.wikipedia.org/wiki/2013_United _States_Senate_special_election_in_New_Jersey.
4. Friedman, Matt. "Lautenberg and Booker's Tortured History Shows Up in Campaign." *Star-Ledger*. Last modified July 29, 2013. https://www.nj.com /politics/2013/07/lautenbergs_and_booker_had_a_tortured_history.html.
5. Halbfinger, David, Raymond Hernandez, and Claire Miller. "Tech Magnates Bet on Booker and His Future." *New York Times*. Last modified August 9, 2013. https://www.nytimes.com/2013/08/07/nyregion/tech -magnates-bet-on-booker-in-web-venture.html.
6. Lach, Eric. "What Will Happen to Cory Booker's Ridiculous Tech Start-Up If He's Elected?" *Talking Points Memo*. Accessed June 23, 2019. https:// talkingpointsmemo.com/muckraker/what-will-happen-to-cory-booker-s -start-up-if-he-s-elected.
7. Kasie Hunt. "Booker Defends Role in Online Startup; Says He's Gone 'Above and Beyond' on Transparency." NBC News. Last modified June 23, 2019. http://firstread.nbcnews.com/_news/2013/08/12/19991544-booker

-defends-role-in-online-startup-says-hes-gone-above-and-beyond-on
-transparency?lite.

8.   Gartland, Michael. "Newark Mayor Cory Booker Pocketed 'confidential'
     Annual Payouts from Law Firm While in Office." *New York Post*. Last mod-
     ified August 11, 2013. https://nypost.com/2013/08/11/newark-mayor-cory
     -booker-pocketed-confidential-annual-payouts-from-law-firm-while-in
     -office/.

9.   *The Stanford Daily*. Last modified February 19, 1992. https://
     stanforddailyarchive.com/cgi-bin/stanford?a=d&d=stanford19920219
     -01.2.16.

10. "Any town, USA (film)." Wikipedia. Last modified July 7, 2017. https://
     en.wikipedia.org/wiki/Anytown,_USA_(film).

11. "Fort Lee Lane Closure Scandal." Wikipedia. Accessed June 23, 2019.
     https://en.wikipedia.org/wiki/Fort_Lee_lane_closure_scandal.

12. Pizzaro, Max. "Lonegan Running for US Senate; Doherty Backing Him."
     Observer. Last modified June 5, 13. https://observer.com/2013/06/lonegan
     -running-for-us-senate-doherty-backing-him/.

13. Lawler, Ryan. "Cory Booker is stepping down from Waywire's Board as the
     company seeks a new CEO." *TechCrunch*. Last modified September 6,
     2013. https://techcrunch.com/2013/09/06/cory-booker-leaves-waywire/.

14. Lawler, Ryan. "Six Months after Acquisition, Magnify Rebrands and
     Re-launches As Waywire." *TechCrunch*. Last modified April 17, 2014.
     https://techcrunch.com/2014/04/17/magnify-waywire-turnover/.

15. Foley, Ryan. "Cory Booker's Tech Startup Failed but Industry Ties Lasted."
     AP NEWS. Last modified May 13, 2019. https://www.apnews.com
     /c5649cccf08a4558a399179fc3e9ccca.

16. Gartland, Michael. "Booker Made $689K from Ex-law Firm While Mayor."
     New York Post. Last modified September 8, 2013. https://nypost.com
     /2013/09/07/booker-made-600k-from-ex-law-firm-while-mayor/.

17. Lonegan, Steve. "Issues." Wayback Machine. Accessed June 23, 2019.
     http://web.archive.org/web/20131016094030/www.loneganforsenate.com
     /issues/.

18. David Giambusso. "Cary Booker, Father of Newark Mayor Cory Booker,
     Dead at 76." *Star-Ledger*. Last modified October 10, 2013. https://www.nj
     .com/politics/2013/10/cory_bookers_father_dead_at_76.html.

19. Booker, Cory. Twitter. Accessed June 23, 2019. https://twitter.com
     /CoryBooker/status/388650494240882688.

THE JUNIOR SENATOR FROM NEW JERSEY

1. "Cory Booker Sworn In As U.S. Senator." *HuffPost*. https://www.huffpost.com/entry/cory-booker-sworn-in-as-us-senator_n_5b571479e4b0cf38668f9abd.

2. "Committee Assignments of the 116th Congress." U.S. Senate. Last modified June 23, 2019. https://www.senate.gov/general/committee_assignments/assignments.htm#BookerNJ.

3. Weigel, David. "Democrats add Harris, Booker to Senate Judiciary Committee." *Washington Post*. Last modified January 9, 2018. https://www.washingtonpost.com/news/powerpost/wp/2018/01/09/democrats-add-harris-booker-to-senate-judiciary-committee/?utm_term=.6be487aae0ad.

4. Stephens, John. "Cory Booker On Medical Marijuana: 'I Want To Go Beyond That.'" *HuffPost*. Last modified December 17, 2012. https://www.huffpost.com/entry/cory-booker-marijuana_n_2274494.

5. Klapper, Ethan. "Cory Booker Slams Drug War." *HuffPost*. Last modified July 16, 2012. https://www.huffpost.com/entry/cory-booker-drug-war_n_1676008.

6. S.2567 - REDEEM Act 113th Congress (2013-2014)

7. Klapper, Ethan. "Cory Booker Slams Drug War." *HuffPost*. Last modified July 16, 2012. https://www.huffpost.com/entry/cory-booker-drug-war_n_1676008.

8. "Chris Christie on Marijuana Legalization: "Never, As Long As I'm Governor." YouTube. April 21, 2014. https://www.youtube.com/watch?v=ydGRT5RN7c4.

9. Kitchenman, Andrew. "Explainer: How New Jersey's Medical Marijuana Law Works." *NJ Spotlight*. Last modified October 14, 2014. https://www.njspotlight.com/stories/14/10/13/explainer-how-new-jersey-s-medical-marijuana-law-works/.

10. Tamari, Jonathan. "Criminal Justice Bill a Major Marker for Cory Booker As 2020 Announcement Looms." Inquirer.com. Last modified December 19, 2018. https://www.inquirer.com/politics/cory-booker-criminal-justice-reform-bill--20181219.html.

11. S.756 - First Step Act of 2018 115th Congress (2017-2018)

12. FIRST STEP Act. Accessed June 24, 2019. https://www.firststepact.org/about.

13. Lartey, Jamiles. "Trump Signs Bipartisan Criminal Justice Overhaul First Step Act into Law." *The Guardian*. Last modified December 21, 2018. https://www.theguardian.com/us-news/2018/dec/21/trump-prison-reform-first-step-act-signed-law.

14. Ho, Vivian. "Criminal Justice Reform Bill Passed by Senate in Rare Bipartisan Victory." *The Guardian*. Last modified December 19, 2018. https://www.theguardian.com/us-news/2018/dec/18/first-step-act-criminal-justice-reform-passes-senate.

15. Cory Booker. "Senate & House Lawmakers Release Updated First Step Act." Cory Booker Senate website. Last modified December 12, 2018. https://www.booker.senate.gov/?p=press_release&id=872.

16. Booker, Cory. Facebook. Accessed June 24, 2019. https://www.facebook.com/corybooker/posts/10156270217357228.

17. Booker, Cory. Twitter. Accessed June 24, 2019. https://twitter.com/CoryBooker/status/818149786847166465.

18. Lesniewski, Niels. "Booker Breaks Precedent by Testifying Against Sessions." *Roll Call*. Last modified January 9, 2017. https://www.rollcall.com/news/politics/booker-breaks-precedent-anti-sessions-testimony.

19. Abadi, Mark. "Cory Booker Thrashes Trump Attorney General Nominee Jeff Sessions in Historic Testimony." *Business Insider*. Last modified January 11, 2017. https://www.businessinsider.com/cory-booker-jeff-sessions-2017-1.

20. Efthim, Rosi. "Transcript: Sen. Cory Booker's Testimony against Sen. Jeff Sessions for Attorney General." *Blue Jersey*. Last modified January 11, 2017. http://www.bluejersey.com/2017/01/transcript-sen-cory-bookers-testimony-against-sen-jeff-sessions-for-attorney-general/.

21. Booker, Cory. Twitter. Accessed June 24, 2019. https://twitter.com/CoryBooker/status/824087184265318401.

22. "Timeline of the Muslim Ban." *ACLU of Washington*. Last modified November 26, 2018. https://www.aclu-wa.org/pages/timeline-muslim-ban.

23. Kiefer, Eric. "New Jersey Protests Trump's Immigration." *Montclair, NJ Patch*. Last modified January 31, 2017. https://patch.com/new-jersey/montclair/north-jersey-protests-trump-s-immigration-order-videos-photos.

24. Booker, Cory. Twitter. Accessed June 24, 2019. https://twitter.com/corybooker/status/825149036160229376.

25. Brennan, John, Owen Proctor, Catherine Carrer, and Keldy Ortiz. "Protests Arise in North Jersey, N.Y.C. Against Trump Order." *North Jersey*. Last modified January 29, 2017. https://www.northjersey.com/story/news/2017/01/29/protests-teaneck-nyc-against-immigration-restrictions/97213378/.

26. "Fiery Speech by Cory Booker at Dulles Airport (1/28/17)." YouTube. January 29, 2017. https://www.youtube.com/watch?v=chT3OAzbhjA.

27. Johnson, Brent. "How Booker, Menendez Say They'll Fight Trump's Recent Orders." *Star-Ledger.* Last modified January 31, 2017. https://www.nj.com/politics/2017/01/booker_menendez_vow_to_fight_trumps_immigration_or.html.

28. Brodesser-Akner, Claude. "The New Trump Travel Ban is Crushing Newark Airport's International Ticket Sales." *Star-Ledger.* Last modified March 13, 2017. https://www.nj.com/politics/2017/03/the_trump_travel_ban_is_offcially_crushing_intl_ai.html.

29. "Looking Back and Fighting Forward on the One-Year Anniversary of Muslim Ban 3.0." National Immigration Law Center. Accessed June 24, 2019. https://www.nilc.org/issues/immigration-enforcement/muslim-ban3-1-year-anniversary-facts/.

30. Giambusso, David. "Storm over North Jersey Waters as Newark Watershed Spends More on Politically Connected Consultants, Critics Demand Reform." *Star-Ledger.* January 29, 2012. Accessed via Nexis.com June 21, 2019.

31. Yi, Karen. "Ex-political Consultant for Newark Watershed Admits Fraud Scheme." *Star-Ledger.* Last modified January 30, 2018. https://www.nj.com/essex/2018/01/ex-consultant_for_newark_watershed_admits_fraud_sc.html.

32. Giambusso, David. "Newark Watershed Dissolves, Leaving City to Manage Water for 500,000 Customers." *New Jersey Star-Ledger.* Last modified March 26, 2013. https://www.nj.com/news/2013/03/newark_watershed_dissolves_lea.html.

33. Gialanella, David. "Former Newark Watershed Counsel Ordered to Pay $59K in Fees Following E-Discovery Dispute." *Law Journal.* Last modified May 1, 2019. https://www.law.com/njlawjournal/2019/05/01/former-newark-watershed-counsel-ordered-to-pay-59k-in-fees-following-e-discovery-dispute/.

34. Giambusso, David. "Thorny Questions about Booker Face Judge in Newark Watershed Case." *Politico.* Last modified March 4, 2016. https://www.politico.com/states/new-jersey/story/2016/03/thorny-questions-about-booker-face-judge-in-newark-watershed-case-031992.

35. Gass, Nick. "Booker: I'm Not Being Vetted for VP." Politico. Last modified June 16, 2016. https://www.politico.com/story/2016/06/cory-booker-no-vice-president-224438.

36. Sherman, Ted. "Accusations Against Booker Dismissed in Newark Watershed Bankruptcy." *Star-Ledger.* Last modified June 23, 2016. https://www.nj.com/news/2016/06/accusations_against_booker_dismissed_in_newark_wat.html.

37. "Cory Booker No Longer Denying He's Being Vetted As Potential Clinton Running Mate." CBS New York. Last modified July 3, 2016. https://newyork.cbslocal.com/2016/07/03/cory-booker-hillary-clinton/.

38. Nuzzi, Olivia. "The Ugly Truth about Cory Booker, New Jersey's Golden Boy." *The Daily Beast.* Last modified October 20, 2014. https://www.thedailybeast.com/the-ugly-truth-about-cory-booker-new-jerseys-golden-boy?ref=scroll.

39. GovTrack.us. "Cory Booker's 2018 Legislative Statistics." GovTrack.us. Accessed June 24, 2019. https://www.govtrack.us/congress/members/cory_booker/412598/report-card/2018.

40. GovTrack.us. "Action for Dental Health Act of 2018 (2018 - S. 3016)." GovTrack.us. Accessed June 24, 2019. https://www.govtrack.us/congress/bills/115/s3016.

41. "9/11 Memorial Act (2018 - S. 3167)." GovTrack.us. Accessed June 24, 2019. https://www.govtrack.us/congress/bills/115/s3167.

42. Eric Bradner. "Cory Booker Eyes 2020 While Crisscrossing the Country for the Midterms." CNN. Last modified June 16, 2018. https://www.cnn.com/2018/06/16/politics/cory-booker-2020-political-travel/index.html.

ANALYSIS: BOOKER'S CHANCES FOR WINNING THE NOMINATION AND PRESIDENCY

1. Haltiwanger, John. "Cory Booker's Half-full Kickoff Rally Could Be Miserable News for the Future of His Campaign." *Business Insider.* Last modified April 14, 2019. https://www.businessinsider.com/cory-booker-half-full-kickoff-rally-bad-sign-for-future-of-campaign-2019-4.

2. Martin, Jonathan. "Who's Running for President in 2020?" *New York Times.* Last modified June 25, 2019. https://www.nytimes.com/interactive/2019/us/politics/2020-presidential-candidates.html.

3. Rebecca Buck. "Booker Says He's Raised More Than $5 Million in First Quarter." CNN. Last modified April 7, 2019. https://www.cnn.com/2019/04/07/politics/cory-booker-fund-raising-numbers/index.html.

4. "Hometown Kickoff: Cory Booker Speech." YouTube. April 14, 2019. https://www.youtube.com/watch?v=G46MrmDIpH8.

5. Booker, Cory. *United: Thoughts on Finding Common Ground and Advancing the Common Good*. 2016. Random House Publishing Group, New York, NY.

6. "Election 2020 - 2020 Democratic Presidential Nomination." *RealClearPolitics*. Accessed June 25, 2019. https://www.realclearpolitics.com/epolls/2020/president/us/2020_democratic_presidential_nomination-6730.html#polls.

7. Shain, Andy. "Warren, Buttigieg Surge in SC 2020 Democratic Presidential Poll As Biden Still Leads." *Post and Courier*. Last modified June 21, 2019. https://www.postandcourier.com/politics/warren-buttigieg-surge-in-sc-democratic-presidential-poll-as-biden/article_0a351cee-8f77-11e9-a29c-9fe60d10303b.html.

8. "South Carolina Primary." Wikipedia. Last modified January 12, 2008. https://en.wikipedia.org/wiki/South_Carolina_primary.

9. Kamisar, Ben. "Biden with Big Lead in New Hampshire Poll." NBC News. Last modified May 9, 2019. https://www.nbcnews.com/card/biden-big-lead-new-hampshire-poll-n1003846.

10. Pindell, James. "Biden, Followed by Sanders and Buttigieg, Leads Among Democrats in N.H. Survey." *Boston Globe*. Last modified April 29, 2019. https://www2.bostonglobe.com/metro/2019/04/29/biden-followed-sanders-and-buttigieg-lead-among-democrats-survey/Gs0gireOuJxvw5SfTTy5wM/story.html.

11. "Election 2020 - Iowa Democratic Presidential Caucus." *RealClearPolitics*. Accessed June 25, 2019. https://www.realclearpolitics.com/epolls/2020/president/ia/iowa_democratic_presidential_caucus-6731.html.

12. Rodrigo, Chris. "Sanders Leads Poll of Young Democrats by Double Digits." *The Hill*. Last modified April 1, 2019. https://thehill.com/homenews/campaign/436675-sanders-leads-poll-of-young-democratic-voters-by-double-digits.

13. Emerson Polling. "Wisconsin 2020: Bernie Sanders Leads Democratic Field; Trump Competitive in General Election." *Reportable*. Accessed June 25, 2019. https://emersonpolling.reportablenews.com/pr/wisconsin-2020-bernie-sanders-leads-democratic-field-trump-competitive-in-general-election.

14. Booker, Cory. "Who Has Endorsed Cory Booker for President?" *Medium*. Last modified April 22, 2019. https://medium.com/@corybooker/who-has-endorsed-cory-booker-for-president-381919f69363.

15. "Election 2020 - General Election: Trump vs. Booker." *RealClearPolitics.* Accessed June 25, 2019. https://www.realclearpolitics.com/epolls/2020 /president/us/general_election_trump_vs_booker-6248.html.

16. Allen, Jonathan. "Why the 2020 Democratic Primary Could Turn into 'Lord of the Flies.'" *NBC News.* Last modified January 24, 2019. https:// www.nbcnews.com/politics/2020-election/why-2020-democratic-primary -could-turn-lord-flies-n961236.

17. Schor, Elana, and Meg Kinnard. "Booker campaign gets 2020 jolt with pushback against Biden." *The Columbus Dispatch.* Last modified June 21, 2019. https://www.dispatch.com/news/20190621/booker-campaign-gets -2020-jolt-with-pushback-against-biden?template=ampart.

18. Easley, Jonathan. "Poll: 60 Percent Say Trump Should Not Be Reelected." *The Hill.* Last modified May 22, 2019. https://thehill.com/homenews /administration/444972-poll-60-percent-say-trump-should-not-be-reelected.